THE
GREAT
TRI-STATE
TORNADO

THE
GREAT
TRI-STATE
TORNADO

JUSTIN HARTER

THE
History
PRESS

Published by The History Press
Charleston, SC
www.historypress.com

First published 2024

Manufactured in the United States

ISBN 9781467157391

Library of Congress Control Number: 2024935316

CONTENTS

ACKNOWLEDGMENTS

Defining the "worst tornado" is a difficult task. In any given state, there are tornado outbreaks and individual tornadoes that are named the "worst" by death toll. Others are measured by time, distance and damage estimates. But one stood out on a list of nationally recognized events. Imagine my surprise when I learned about the tri-state tornado of 1925 for the first time after I had lived in the Midwest for over thirty-five years. "Why have I never heard of this?" I wondered. No one I knew or spoke to knew anything about it either. Thus began the desire to write the book I wanted to read about this storm, which seemingly held nearly all the worst records for time, distance, wind speed, injuries, destruction, costs and deaths.

The solitary hours at my desk tapping away on my keyboard notwithstanding, *The Great Tri-State Tornado* was not a solitary effort. Assembling this book would not have been possible without the help of countless reporters who chronicled news stories before, during and after the storm, to say nothing of the efforts of unknown hundreds who scanned, digitized and organized those records.

I want to thank the people who sat down with me for interviews, including Jane Sims, Sam Lashley at the Indianapolis National Weather Service Office and historian staff and volunteers working at the Lincoln Library in Illinois, the Indiana State Library and a dozen county societies across Missouri, Illinois and Indiana. All of them allowed me to impose on their schedules—sometimes multiple times—to ask questions. And I'd like to thank my husband, Jeremiah, whose support is immeasurable. His trust and faith in me are ingrained within these pages more than he realizes. To everyone I spoke to in search of clues and help for this book: thank you.

AUTHOR'S NOTES

Much about the tri-state tornado of 1925 remains a mystery. Despite all the best reporting at the time and all the science discovered in the last century, there are periods of the storm during which no one saw or could survey it. Like veterans after a horrible war, the people who survived the storm seldom wanted to discuss it and have long since died. Their children with any memories—even the memories of a child from the age of eight to twelve at the time of the storm—have also died or faded with time.

In the last one hundred years, the facts and fiction about the storm have twisted together like the clouds on March 18, 1925. For many who were in the storm, their memories were shrouded in fear and anxiety. They often simply said, "It got really dark, then loud, and then it was all over."

In piecing together this story, I relied on extensive news records, journals, government reports and weather records and data that have since been archived by researchers at Purdue University and elsewhere. I also relied on numerous interviews conducted by me and others. When information from one source conflicted with another, I judged the truth based on a credible authority, like which source was in the best position to know the facts or had the most reliable records. If those differences remained uncertain, I chose to believe the version of the story that was most corroborated by others and which events or series of events best fit with the science and known facts.

Some of what happened in the storm's path and aftermath will never be known with certainty. I have tried to fill in some gaps by suggesting reasonable or consistent events with the evidence, science, testimony or expert opinion of the people involved.

As best as I and anyone know at the time of this writing, the following pages are the best available truth about the storm.

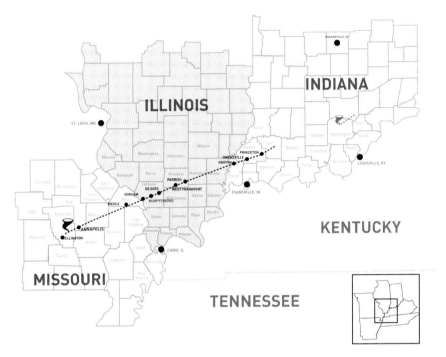

The track of the tri-state tornado across the Midwest. *Author's collection.*

1

REYNOLDS COUNTY, MISSOURI

ELLINGTON

Sam Flowers thought nothing much of the unseasonably warm weather on Wednesday, March 18, 1925. Flowers walked outside to fifty-five-degree air and bright gray skies in Poplar Bluff, Missouri. Only just before daybreak did a few light showers amble across the Ozark Foothills. For a while, Flowers thought the weather might have been clearing up.[1]

The forty-nine-year-old Redford, Missouri farmer had just celebrated his birthday two days earlier with his wife, Mary Adaline. The couple's twenty-six-year-long marriage delivered them four sons and three daughters, aged six to twenty-four.[2]

As Sam began his journey home from town in the drizzle, a low-pressure system started skidding west out of Kansas and Arkansas. It had been an unusually warm, dry winter in much of the Mississippi and Ohio Valleys.[3] A brief cold spell in the first two weeks of March had lost its grip, signaling winter's last gasp. Now, it felt like spring again, leaving Sam and farmers like him all around Reynolds County uneasy about the dry year. They looked to the skies with appreciation, as they needed the rain to soften the ground for tilling.[4]

At the Flowers family farmstead in Redford, just outside Ellington, Missouri, Mary stood at the counter gazing out the kitchen window. She and the rest of the Flowers family expected Sam home from Poplar Bluff, sixty miles south, later that day. The skies grew dull, and gloomy rain clouds moved in overhead. Mary also appreciated the much-needed rain but already felt exhausted thinking about the day's damp work tending to the cows, hogs and chickens and other soggy chores.

Reynolds County was booming in 1925. More people lived in the county then than at any other time. Over ten thousand residents called this area of the Ozark Foothills home, including the Flowers family, who moved north from Kentucky in search of prosperity. The area's workable soil and plentiful lead mines seemed full of possibilities. Redford still comprised only a few dozen scattered farms in the orbit of Ellington, the largest and proudest town in the county, with several hundred residents.[5]

So proud were Ellington's residents and leaders that they decided they should be prepared for any emergency if one should come. With fire being the primary safety concern (and without public waterworks or fire hydrants), it was decreed that everyone should buy a fire extinguisher and keep it loaded and handy "for instant use." So, that's what they did. Nearly half the men in the city purchased a chemical extinguisher and declared themselves volunteer firemen, ready to spring forth and protect their town. "Ellington has the most unique fire department in the State of Missouri," wrote one journalist visiting from Poplar Bluff in early March 1925. The journalist dutifully reported that half the town's men were part of the brigade with just as many automobiles.[6]

When the two-story home of Tobe Fitzgerald caught fire earlier that month, the reporter assumed it was doomed as soon as the local mill sounded the fire whistle. When the town's men heard the whistle from the factories, they dashed to their automobiles and rushed toward the billowing smoke. The roof of the house was a roaring furnace when the first volunteers arrived. The lucky reporter, who happened to be in the right place at the right time, watched in awe. "In less than three minutes the fire brigade—in automobiles—was on the scene and the blaze was extinguished in the proverbial three shakes of a lamb's tail," he wrote. Another fire that threatened the Woolworth building in town was suppressed in an equally impressive amount of time.

The *St. Louis Globe-Democrat* later republished the story about the town's brave volunteer firefighters, giving the people of Ellington regional recognition. Things were looking up for Ellington. Jobs were plentiful, and the soil and mines seemed rich and bountiful. People were buying automobiles and telephones and all sorts of new technology. Taxes were low, the town had $500 in the bank, the county was growing and everyone in Ellington was hopeful for the best and prepared for the worst.[7]

Sam Flowers, like Ellington, had changed a lot over the last few years. He was now a sturdy straw-haired man of thirty with a rather hard mouth and an enormously powerful body. Two shining blue eyes had established dominance over his face and gave him the appearance that he was always leaning aggressively forward.

Sam Flowers did not have an automobile, like about half of the people in Ellington. His journey home on horseback through the rough and sparse countryside took most of the day. Leaving Poplar Bluff at daybreak, Sam's horse Babe trotted up and down the rolling hills, past the big oaks and maples lining the burnt-red dirt roads. Still leafless from the winter, the trees' bare limbs rustled back and forth, rubbing against one each other in the gentle breeze and rain. Familiar with the roads, Sam kept his blue eyes sharp with concern as an occasional car passed along. He expected to arrive home by supper.

The rain began falling more steadily through the morning. A warm front that was pushing up from the southeast hung awkwardly over the county. It was muggy in the southern half of Iron County, but in the northern reaches, the skies were gray, and light rain was falling. Temperatures were also slightly cooler north of Ellington, even as daylight warmed the atmosphere above the clouds. A low-pressure system had formed a day earlier over southeast Colorado and was now swirling just southwest of Sam. Torrential rain, hail and thunderstorms boomed across parts of Kansas and Arkansas that morning and were now moving into Missouri.

Sam reached Ellington around noon, just as his horse needed a drink. L.W. Sanders, the town's barber, had just moved his shop behind the post office and was busy cutting hair when Sam hitched up nearby. Glancing around the familiar town, Sam watched as people milled around the Grant Hotel, which had just been sold to new owners the week prior.[8] Local bankers and mineworkers headed to lunch. Women caught between bursts of rain and short on groceries hoisted their dresses in a useless attempt to avoid the mud.

Sam's black hair and muscular shoulders dripped from the day's fine rain. As the hum of the townspeople walking around surrounded Sam, he stood, looking around the sloppy streets as Babe drank from a trough. Sam could feel the temperature rising. Buoyed by a warm front pumping warm air up from the south, the air was about sixty degrees, the humidity was high amid the passing rain showers and the wind blew steadily, with gusts reaching up twenty or thirty miles per hour. As Babe bobbed up and down in the trough, which was overflowing from the morning's rain, the atmosphere's ingredients of warm, cool, dry and wet air roiled together to spawn a classic supercell thunderstorm on the horizon.

Sam knew all the telltale signs of a storm from the sky and terrain from growing up in Kentucky. The air smelled like spring showers. If the rain came down hard enough, seeing the path ahead on horseback would be too difficult. It was nothing too ominous, but he ditched the idea of riding across open fields in favor of the relative safety of well-trodden roads.

With darkening clouds chasing them home and to the northeast, Babe and Sam set out for home again. Sam crested a hill at a clearing and moved out of town along the country road near Logan Creek. Back over his shoulder, hundreds of acres of trees and woods in the distance began to sway back and forth under an aggressively gray sky, as if waving for help, as the wind picked up speed.

It was around 12:30 p.m. on Wednesday when the raindrops began to swell. Sam and Babe were only about twelve miles from home when the rain began blowing in intermittent sheets across their path, stinging their cheeks and eyes.[9] The signs from the sky brimmed with anger. The storm clouds behind Sam collided in a nexus of low pressure, high pressure, warm and moist air and cool, dry air. The unusually stark warm front split the atmosphere across the Midwest into rainy conditions and air that was as much as ten degrees cooler than the warmer, dryer air a mere ten to twenty miles north of its southern border. The supercell thunderstorm tracked along the warm front, sputtering and twisting itself into a tornado.

Neighboring farms usually created a helpful quilt of recognizable fence posts and neat hedgerows for easy navigation. But now, they were barely visible to Sam in the rain. A low cloud descended behind him, steadily urging Sam and Babe onward. Nearby pine trees brushed against the sky's darkening canvas. The rain advanced like a tremendous wall of water, slamming against Sam's face and drenched clothes.

Sam was confident he could make it home to secure his horses and shelter from the pending storm alongside Mary and his children. He gripped the reins tightly and raced Babe at full gallop, pushing hard to get ahead of the storm.

Sam rode Babe as quickly as she could go after already traveling a rigorous fifty miles, and hailstones the size of quarters began falling from the sky. The force and fury of God's thunder, rain and hail rumbled directly over them, turning the road into a thick slurry of mud and ice.

The rain wrapped around them. Sam judged nothing about the ominous, dark gray sky that seemed worth hunkering down or stopping at a neighbor's farmhouse for. Sam had seen countless storms and knew the signs of a tornado. Still, the clouds drooped lower, and sporadic lightning forced the sky to flash black and white as thunder rolled out of the sky.

Sam didn't know it, but this storm had already spawned a tornado across Kansas, Oklahoma and Arkansas before dawn that morning. Rain and hail the size of peas and small eggs pelted the western Missouri countryside all morning.

Back at the farmhouse, Mary brought the children in for lunch as the rain started to fall. The skies darkened. The stove that kept the house warm overnight now simmered a low heat. The family stared out over the hillside, wondering if Sam had gotten caught up in this mess or if he had taken shelter somewhere around Ellington. With no phone or telegraph at the farm, Mary couldn't ask anyone in town if they had seen her husband yet.

A little after 1:00 p.m., just over Sam Flower's shoulder, the atmosphere came into alignment, and a mighty wedge-shaped funnel descended like an anvil and contacted the ground. Whenever he looked back, Sam could still see nothing but gray clouds. The rain was everywhere at once, and hailstones forced his gaze down. Above the occasional rumble of thunder and constant whirr of the storm's wind, posts and timber joined the hail and rain thrashing down toward the ground. As Sam could barely open his eyes against the stinging rain, the wind pushed hard against his entire body.

Forced to dismount from Babe, Sam began walking with no place to go and nowhere to shelter except against each the horse's sturdy frame. Sam and Babe inched along the road one step at a time, holding each other close, hail crunching under their feet.

Amid the pressure to escape, Sam considered returning to Ellington until the storm rolled over. He reasoned the town was closer than his farm, but it was clear the storm had caught him in a far more dangerous situation than he expected.

He still could not make out the shape of a funnel cloud. The wind blew so furiously that the grass lay down in complete submission. Before Sam could think about his situation any longer, a chunk of wood came hurtling through the air and bashed him in the back of the head, killing him instantly and throwing his body a short distance from the road.

At the farmhouse about ten miles away, the sky boomed around Mary and the family like a cannonade, shaking the doors and windows. Not taking any chances, Mary and the eldest kids scooped the young ones into the corner of the house. The wind vibrated the doors as they anxiously waited for the storm to pass. The rain kept slamming down as the sky turned black, stretching in every direction for miles. For a while, it must have felt like God was stomping on the ground around them.

Then, almost as quickly as the sky had darkened, it lightened up again. The rain straightened out, with the occasional small hailstone rolling along the ground. Mary and the children opened the doors and stepped out of the house to find hunks of trees and timber all around them. The farm appeared to suffer minimal damage. Still, there was no sign of Sam. Fearful but trusting in Sam's ability to stay safe, the family retreated inside the home to wait out the rain.

Soaked from mane to hoof and exhausted from riding sixty miles, a riderless Babe trotted onto the Flowerses' farm later that afternoon, as she had done routinely hundreds of times before. Worried and fearing the worst for Sam, Mary and her eldest sons, Orval, Harley, Thomas and Marvin, set out door to door to organize a small search party.

Ten miles southwest, in Ellington, people turned out of their homes to assess the destruction. Most people's properties came out unscathed, except for wind damage to roofs and fences and fallen timbers. Wondering where the damage came from, volunteer firemen bolted into their automobiles and set out in all directions, curious to discover if a tornado had touched down and if they could offer help.

All afternoon and evening, volunteers and neighbors checked on each other and the outlying farms and cleared trees from roads. As daylight dwindled, reports began to spread around Reynolds County of barns, fences, orchards and timber that had been felled and strewn around. As nightfall demanded the use of headlamps and lanterns, the parties learned Len Rayfield's house in Spring Valley, just a short distance from Sam, was thoroughly brushed away.

Word about the pursuit of Sam spread as search party members met up at the Flowerses' farm. Volunteers drove carefully up and down roads between Redford and Ellington until a search party discovered Sam's body around 4:00 a.m. the next day.[10]

His body was lying just off the road, where the storm had left him. Leaves and brush all around his body lay flattened. The opinion of the family and searchers was that there definitely was a tornado, and Sam Flowers, along with Len Rayfield's house, were directly in its path.

They didn't know it yet, but Sam was the first casualty of a tornado that would go on to kill 694 more people over 219 long midwestern miles.

2

IRON COUNTY, MISSOURI

ANNAPOLIS AND LEADANNA

Most of the significant changes and events in the history of Annapolis and nearby Leadanna, Missouri, were the expansions of the mines. The Annapolis lead mine opened in 1919, and by 1925, about 9,500 people lived in Iron County. Men came from Missouri, Illinois and Kentucky to start new lives, undaunted by the challenging labor before them. They lived in gaunt wooden houses on rugged terrain that sloped west toward Sutton Branch Creek. Whatever land remained was covered by sweetgum, silver maple, ash, elm and Bradford pear trees.

The Annapolis lead mine extended 450 feet below ground, with several hundred feet of lateral lines sprawling in all directions. As raw materials and galena—the natural mineral form of lead—were lifted to the surface on conveyors and pulleys, the crushed and concentrated waste was often disposed of nearby, where it then leached into the creek and some underground water wells.[11]

The families who settled in the area endured conditions as harsh as their drinking water. Lead miners were skilled and hearty and pulled hundreds of tons of lead from the Earth's veins, but accidents were common. Mining was risky, and few miners lived past the age of fifty. If they could survive the dangers and debris of the Earth, silicosis caused by drilling and dust usually stealthily suffocated their lungs.

Despite the drawbacks of arid land, hot summers, harsh winters and suffocating work, the place charmed many who called it home. Aboveground, women and children helped clear the land for modest gardens and buildings between the usual trappings of small-town living. People enjoyed bird walks, and children ran in open fields. Boys courted young ladies, people gathered at the hotel and diner to gossip and everyone worshiped weekly at church.

The Missouri Pacific Railroad opened a train station in Annapolis soon after the mines opened, connecting the area to the rest of the world. A northbound Missouri Pacific train, no. 32, was on its way to Annapolis from Arcadia on March 18, 1925, with passengers who expected to arrive midday. Another train, no. 33, was supposed to arrive shortly after.

Several passenger trains bound for St. Louis and Chicago rumbled daily, as did industrial cars operated by the Missouri Pacific, which were primarily used to cart ore, lead and galena away from the area. The trains brought in more people as quickly as they carried the earth out. As a result, one of the biggest changes in the area came to the public schools in the early 1920s. "The rural schools of Southeast Missouri have advanced very rapidly the past two years, and much of this advancement has been made during the last twelve months," wrote local school supervisor O.E. McGee in early 1925.[12] A series of meetings between many of the region's parents and teachers in 1924 and 1925 highlighted the schools' problems. "Much has been done to better equip schools" because of those meetings, McGee wrote. Indeed, schools across southern and southeastern Missouri were undertaking advanced new school-building programs. Communities built new schools with better lighting, heating and paint. "At no time in the history of this section have the teachers been giving so much time and effort to their professional advancement," added McGee.

Around seventy Annapolis schoolchildren were among the beneficiaries of these improvements. The two-story Annapolis School beamed on the western edge of town. It was constructed of sturdy, modern brick masonry and had just been filled with new maps, globes, blackboards, charts and books for the 1925 school year. The U.S. flag waved proudly outside its single white door.

Around 12:30 p.m. on March 18, the flag briefly came to rest peacefully against the school's flagpole. The weather had turned warm for the last several days. It was about sixty degrees as Superintendent Roy Taylor stood on top of a small stoop covered by a jutting triangular roof and watched as the children played on the hillside.

For most of the morning, the children enjoyed the unseasonable warmth. The occasional growl of thunder lazily rolled over the hills from the west a little before noon, but the scattered rain that had spread over the area held off around recess. The kids scampered merrily in the open field. No one

The Annapolis School, Iron County, Missouri. *1925 Missouri Annual Reports of Public Schools.*

thought the sky was more alarming than it was during any other early spring thunderstorm. But the tornado that had spun down just east of Ellington fifteen minutes earlier was barreling toward Annapolis and Leadanna.

Three teachers, Miss Louise Curry, Miss Lillian Oller and Miss Gladys Lovelace, joined Superintendent Taylor on the stoop.[13] They chatted among themselves as they took turns glancing over at the kids roughhousing. As students played in the field, the air moved again as towering cumulus clouds dragged great shadows across the land. At first, students were curious, and the boys excitedly tossed their hats into the air to see how far a gust of wind could carry them. But their curiosity changed with the sky. Looking up over the distance, many students fretted as the sun vanished. Suddenly and without warning, sheets of rain and hail began to plink off the schoolhouse roof and grounds. Noticing the trees were shaking more violently in the distance, Miss Curry called the students into the building around 1:00 p.m. The new windows that let in so much light to help children see and read now served as portholes to look out over the blackening skies.

The German immigrant women on Annapolis's western end had noticed the thunder that rumbled in the distance since about noon. As tornadoes move across land, their color changes based on the soil beneath them. Most start the same color as the clouds they are birthed from. Denser clouds block out more sunlight, and as the funnels kick up dust, dirt and soil from the surface, the sky can change hue within seconds.

Treading outside around 12:30 p.m., as their husbands worked in the mines, the women noticed the sky was a deep brown and simmering red

Downtown Annapolis, Missouri, shortly after the storm. *Annapolis, MO: Centennial publication, Iron County, Missouri Historical Society, 1971.*

color. The low rumbles of thunder and occasional breeze encouraged most of them to pull their laundry off the lines. They sensed a storm was coming but could not see a tornado. Most thought the wind had picked up enough of the iron-rich soil to appear more like a dust storm.

In the middle of Annapolis, traveling salesman C.E. Pyrtle was sitting in his car on Main Street, rifling through papers and receipts.[14] He had also noticed the sky's unusual hue but was hurriedly preparing for his next sale. Dozens of shops and doors were waiting to be visited. Missouri State Highway Commission teamster Merle Stewart was clearing debris along a stretch of road connecting Annapolis and Leadanna.[15] The road was used by the trucks and workers that clambered between mines and railyards.

In Leadanna, thirty-three-year-old Osero Kelley; his twenty-one-year-old wife, Nellie; and fifteen-year-old son, Paul, were at home doing chores.[16] An electrical engineer at the Annapolis Lead Company, Osero wasn't among the sixty-five other men in the mines that day. His work kept him on the surface.

With shocking force and intensity, hail began to pummel the ground around 1:15 p.m. Mrs. John Thomas, the mother of Mrs. Kelley, looked out her kitchen window to the southwest and noticed a black, funnel-shaped cloud. Momentarily frozen and unsure of what to do, she turned to the other window, only to witness her chicken house fly by and the barn crash down.

The house she was standing in shook violently. To secure the door, which began rattling on its hinges, Mrs. Thomas put a chair against it, but the wind blew the door open, sweeping her and the chair across the floor. The tornado that had started just east of Ellington was now relentlessly focused on Annapolis and Leadanna for the next four minutes.

Students shrieked with fear at the Annapolis School as windows revealed nothing but dark gray fog rolling into a black morass outside. They likely could have confused the dark clouds for smoke had it not been for the rain and hail. Fearing the windows might blow in or out—no one was sure which—from the strengthening winds, Miss Curry ushered her two dozen students around her desk at the front of the room.

Salesman C.E. Pyrtle was still sitting on Main Street in his automobile when the cyclone came on so suddenly that there was no time to react. The tornado was so vast that Pyrtle noticed the sky darken almost simultaneously to the east and west, as if enveloping him with two outstretched arms. Before he could react, the violent air pulled him away from his car, pinned him to the ground and pummeled his head with hunks of timber. He awoke five minutes later, dazed and confused about how he had ended up in the middle of the street. He told one newspaper reporter, "I saw only three or four houses where there had been three hundred to four hundred. The schoolhouse was standing on the edge of the town."[17]

The remains of the Annapolis Lead Co., Annapolis, Missouri. *Annapolis, MO: Centennial publication, Iron County, Missouri Historical Society, 1971.*

W.E. Lemley, a tie inspector for the Ruth Lumber Company of Poplar Bluff, Missouri, was eating lunch in the local diner when the storm struck. "The roof went off first, and then all four sides were swept away," he told a journalist. Miraculously, he said, "I was left sitting on the floor with nothing around me." His plate and unfinished lunch were untouched.[18]

William Voyles, a general storekeeper, crawled under a pile of dry goods and clothes, figuring the soft merchandise would cushion him from any debris. When the tornado came, he escaped unhurt, despite the building crumpling on top of him.[19] Another nearby restaurant owner survived by climbing into an icebox just as the winds ripped away at the walls.[20]

Across Annapolis and Leadanna, the mills, machinery, tipples and buildings that formed the town's economic foundation cracked and swayed under the mighty winds. Twenty-one homes owned by the Leadanna Lead Company were demolished. Osero Kelley, an electrical engineer, died when he was thrown against a tree and struck by falling debris. His wife was also struck in the head and suffered severe cuts and a broken leg. A similar fate befell Merle Stewart, a highway worker, when swirling lumber cracked against his head and torso, killing him instantly.

The Annapolis School continued to hold together, thanks to its location just outside of the rest of town and its sturdy new construction. None of the children were hurt, but nearly every window shattered against the wind, and a portion of the roof was torn off.[21] Nearby, the son of John Havener, a three-year-old child who was too young to be in school, was picked up from his family's house and carried a quarter of a mile before he was dropped to the ground, uninjured.[22]

Mr. H. Robbs was sitting on the Missouri Pacific's no. 32, waiting for the St. Louis–bound no. 33 to pass by so he could leave. The no. 32 had departed Poplar Bluff that morning and was quietly waiting at the Annapolis train station when the brunt of the twister passed overhead. Passengers in the rear cars sat helplessly as their windows blew in on them, and they wondered if the train would be blown from its tracks.[23] Passengers howled and shrieked in fear as sixty-mile-per-hour winds punched the sides of the cars. The extreme pressure changes and updraft of the tornado's nearly mile-wide interior almost lifted the cars from the tracks, but it failed to secure its grip as cars and bodies lurched violently.

Hail the size of potatoes lashed at the train's roofs and windows. Frightened passengers clung to their seats as they watched the roof of a nearby house be cleanly peeled off like a bedsheet. Train engineer Robbs encouraged everyone to remain calm.[24] The lights went out, the sky grew darker and the train's conductor ducked under the engine car's windows. Four minutes felt like four hours.

The Annapolis train station shook as the nails and carpentry that held it together were torn asunder. With the storm boiling overhead, W.C. Gunther, the station's ticket agent-operator, sat at his window. Patrons inside began running in every direction and screaming, groping for an exit or the relative safety of something sturdy. Timbers and support beams collapsed on waiting passengers.

"I had a narrow escape," Gunther recalled. He remained uninjured behind his ticket bay window after the storm passed. Gunther took stock of himself and realized, as if by providence, the only thing left standing was the frame window and table where he sat. The station was leveled to kindling. A coal-burning stove in the corner had toppled over, releasing piping-hot coals and cinders into the debris. Gunther spotted a working spigot, filled his cash drawer and splashed the fire, extinguishing it before it could incinerate the building's remains.[25]

The no. 33 train, bound for St. Louis, had come through and just passed by to find a town cleanly swept away. Anything that wasn't blown away was left in pieces, as if imploded by dynamite. Expecting to find help, Robbs and the conductor on the no. 32 train set out from Annapolis. For ten miles, they encountered nothing but scarred earth, felled trees and not a single standing telegraph or telephone pole. Annapolis was completely paralyzed and disconnected from the rest of the world; only the no. 32 and no. 33 train passengers knew about the situation there.

The tornado was over in four minutes. Rain poured for fifteen minutes afterward until the skies began to clear; the wind shifted, the humidity dropped and the temperatures cooled into the low fifties. In Annapolis and Leadanna, four people were dead, including engineers Merle Stewart and Osero Kelley. Twenty-five people suffered injuries, including sales agent Pyrtle, who sustained a slight concussion. Only seven houses remained standing, along with the school and a garage. In Leadanna, thirty-three of the forty-five houses and all the mine structures and equipment lay in a heap.

Six hundred newly homeless people would have to endure the wet and cold until help could arrive. For now, the only hospitality came from ticket agent Gunther, who pushed open the doors to some of the extra boxcars that remained upright on a sidetrack so wet residents to stand out of the chilly rain.[26]

For the men who were working underground at the Annapolis Mine, their curiosity was aroused when their flickering lights abruptly shut off.

Emerging from their relatively quiet underground worksite, they found their town had vanished. Pushing some debris away from the mine entrance, the men rushed out into town, hollering the names of their children and wives. "Watch out for the downed power line!" men yelled. Anonymous voices boomed, "Be careful where you step! The telegraph wires are down under here!" Many returned to where their homes once stood, only to find the remains of another house piled on top. Others became disoriented without the familiar pattern of landmarks to guide them. Hearing screams for help from the tiny lungs of babies and toddlers under debris, men heaved and pulled at beams, timber, sheet metal and shingles with their bare hands, yelling for loved ones, only to find they were digging under a neighbor's house.

Of the few houses that were left standing in the center of town, one belonged to a sickly Ms. Collins. She had been unable to move around for some time.[27] Despite her house being left intact, a fire from the restaurant next door began to spread and devoured her home as men rushed in to rescue her. More fires flashed into the afternoon and evening sky. What started with a brown and simmering red sky turned upside down as mud and fire stained the earth a murky brown and red.

Passengers on the no. 32 train headed onward, following just behind and south of the storm's path until they turned north, away from the twister. Nothing but damaged trees and hailstones the size of bird eggs were visible for miles.

Twenty miles north, in Arcadia, Missouri, a conductor bounded down the steps and rushed into the depot with the news from Annapolis.[28] Unsure where the storm was now or how much damage had been done in Annapolis, the reaction from the people of Arcadia was a mixture of excitement and confusion. People began loading into their automobiles to see for themselves. Telegraph operators began flashing the news in all directions, attempting to pinpoint areas still receiving messages. Likely assuming the tornado, like most tornadoes, had been short-lived and already crawled back into the sky, operators failed to signal ahead any warning that a storm might be approaching.

3

ENTERING ILLINOIS

GORHAM, ILLINOIS

Katy White kept her eyes on the griddle in front of her that was sizzling with beef, hash and potatoes, occasionally glancing down the hall and out the door, toward the countryside locals called "Little Egypt."

Amid European settlement at the turn of the nineteenth century, settlers compared the region's proximity to the Mississippi River and fertile farmland to that of the Nile Valley. Towns with names like Cairo, Thebes and Lebanon became European settlements alongside Native villages. By the time of the Civil War, the name had stuck, and enslaved people talked about traveling to "Canaan," the land of milk and honey, as parts of the Underground Railroad wove north from Kentucky, Missouri and points farther south.

Gorham was situated in Jackson County with not much more than one hundred homes and fertile farms, a post office, Wallace's Restaurant and a few shops for necessities. Life there was hard but manageable. Gorham was isolated from the world except for the rail corridor that carried passenger and heavy industrial railcars from Missouri, north across Jackson County toward nearby Murphysboro and south along the Mississippi River.

On the western edge of town, sixty-eight-year-old Sarah Bean and her seventy-year-old husband, Harvey, sat quietly in their home. The couple married when Sarah was seventeen and Harvey twenty. They descended from the sort of pioneer stock that made life in the tiny village of Gorham charming.[29] Mrs. Bean witnessed an avalanche of smoke and debris around 2:15 p.m. First, a cow flew by as if it had wings. Then a thousand other things filled the air. Boards, stoves, trees, poles, cans, clothes, entire sides of houses and roofs were all torn from the earth.

Elsewhere, Judith Cox had a long list of errands for the day. Before leaving the house, she tucked her husband's paycheck into her coat pocket; then she looked at the time and dashed out the door. Her husband, a Missouri Pacific foreman, was out of town for the day. To liven up the afternoon, she ducked into Wallace's Restaurant to visit with her friends Mary Clark and Louise "Lulu" Moschenrose. The three sipped coffee and enjoyed lunch amid all the midday chatter about their kids and the day's gloomy weather.

Back in the kitchen, Katy White stared down at her sizzling griddle of potatoes and beef. The rain had started an hour or two earlier. Everyone glanced outside at the occasional person ambling down the street, soaked but unbothered. Finishing up her lunch, Judith looked out the large restaurant windows and noticed the rain coming down harder.

"I'd better get home," she told Mary and Lulu. "The rain is picking up," she added, gathering up her coat and purse from the table. "I still have to get to the bank to deposit this check." She got up and threw her coat on over her shoulders.

Walking toward the thin screen door, she opened it to find the sky had darkened into a great wall of rain. Her eyes widened. "It's a cyclone!" she cried, looking back at the dining room. Small bits of rocks, hail and other debris began pelting the windows.

Hearing the commotion and wondering what was happening, Katy abandoned the griddle and walked toward the front door, only to see murky water churning in the air, packed with debris and mud. The force of the wind deepened to a ceaseless roar. All Katy could see was what looked like impenetrable smoke billowing past the open door and windows that must have looked more like a wildfire outside.

Surging with instinct, Judith exclaimed, "I must reach my two children!" Mary and Lulu stood up from the table to get a better look outside, their lungs filling with fear and raw adrenaline. Judith put her head down against the whipping lashes of sixty- and seventy-mile-per-hour winds and pushed out the door, but the storm denied her the chance to leave, as it stung her face with rain and ripped her coat off her body. Judith was powerless to control her body as the front wall of the tornado entered Gorham and banished her back into the restaurant. The relentless howl against the walls drowned out the restaurant's creaking frame and the patrons' blistering shrieks inside. All three women and Katy were immediately blown back and pinned against the hot stove.

The restaurant's frame groaned under increasing winds and twisting updrafts until it began to splinter and collapse. The fire inside the stove seared the women's skin immediately. Flush with oxygen, the fire flashed upward, like faces in a nightmare. Rain, dirt and thousands of pounds of tiny particles of sand, timber and debris pelted Judith's body as she struggled to open her eyes. Worries about her children flashed in Judith's mind. Squinting to her side and praying for a chance to stay in this world a little longer, Judith could not make out the sizable figure of anyone or anything around.[30] She had survived, but for now, all she could do was wait.

At the Gorham School, Alice Sumner, fourteen, was sitting in her classroom when a young boy remarked how dark the sky was becoming. Students rushed to the windows to the consternation of their teacher, who promptly ordered them back to their seats. Just as the children returned to their desks, the outside world, as described by another student, was "dark as night."

Alice fixed her gaze out the windows, searching for a clue about what could cause this much ruckus. She reasoned that it did not sound like a tornado, but the school's flag blew at a near-perfect horizontal pitch in the wind, as if it were hardened like wood. As Alice tried to refocus on her teacher, the sinister darkness enveloped the school.

Suddenly and without warning, the tornado's force blew the school's walls and windows in on the students, sending shards of glass into their tender faces and bodies. The screams of children stricken with fear and panic were clipped and rendered inaudible as the tornado ripped the school to splinters like two grand bulls charging into each other. Within seconds, the school's floor melted away as students who were clinging to their chairs and desks collapsed into the basement.

The tornado was three-quarters of a mile wide, but no one could see a funnel. Instead, only a churning, angry fog with streaks of muddy Mississippi River water whipping forcefully in all directions came barreling down. Every building in Gorham was destroyed or rendered uninhabitable within a few minutes.

As residents picked themselves up in the moments after the storm's frightful devastation, the roar of the wind was replaced by the screams of survivors. Most of the buildings that were not wholly blown asunder wilted and seemed to have been imploded under the force of side winds and updraft. Despite the rain, the air was awash with fear and adrenaline. Hailstones the size of potatoes and baseballs lay on the ground alongside the victims, including Lulu Moschenrose and Katy White at Wallace's Restaurant. Both women were crushed to death under the weight of what was the restaurant. Joe Moschenrose, a local butcher and Lulu's brother, ran into the remnants of Wallace's Restaurant to find Judith Cox alive under debris that was being held up by a surviving cow that had been blown into the restaurant. After some of the debris was lifted off the cow, it trotted off in search of quieter pastures. Joe did not know it yet, but his brothers Andrew and Edward Moschenrose lay dead across town.

Rainwater seeped into everything. Inside the First National Bank, where Judith had intended to deposit the family's paycheck, cashier Ernest Schwartz crawled out of the bank's vault. Just the day before, his mother had told him to never go in there for fear that he would be trapped alongside an antitheft air poisoning device. But as the storm approached, Schwartz ignored his mother's advice, grabbed every coin and dollar bill he could and fled into the vault. Only twenty dollars was left unaccounted for. His mother later reported to the Benton, Illinois *Evening News* on March 21, she was "tickled pink" he disregarded her advice to never go inside the vault.

Everyone in town, including the thirty-seven dead, were caked with mud that had been so forcibly thrown against their bodies, only their eyes appeared clean until they closed them. Those who had forced their eyelids open against the storm were rendered blind, usually for months and sometimes permanently. The clocks that remained amid the debris stood still at 2:25 p.m.

Survivors found landings and crawled out of basements if they could. Basements shielded some residents from flying debris but trapped others under the wreckage and wires. Those who stepped outside found an unrecognizable landscape glazed in terror.

"Watch out for wires!" people yelled into the street as they tread carefully to avoid the sparks from downed telegraph poles. What had not been completely blown away was left as exposed nails, glass and splintered shards of unrecognizable metal. Despite taking careful steps, dozens of people inadvertently stepped on shards of glass or nails that pierced their shoes and feet. The town's lone doctor, suffering from a broken collarbone, unearthed his bag and administered inoculations to patients as quickly as they were dying from their injuries.

Judith Cox, now free from the debris and cow, found her raincoat—complete with her husband's paycheck still in the pocket—on a tree branch and ran toward the school, where most of the children had been dumped into the basement. The building was only four years old and was now a furrowed shell of bricks, mortar and cinder blocks that held up the once-three-story school.[31]

She found children walking in a daze, crying, screaming and surging with fear and pain. Mothers and fathers across town came running to the school, bleeding and limping from their own wounds. They found some of their children dead; overcome with grief, they began to weep openly on the scarred ground. The cold rain dripped over their shoulders and hair, providing them no relief. Judith Cox found her two teenage children alive and pelted with mud, splinters and sand that looked like it had been injected under the skin.

The train depot that served as Gorham's economic engine was gone. Eighteen boxcars had been blown over and rendered unusable for anything other than makeshift shelter, much like their disconnected neighbors in Annapolis discovered. The entire village that four hundred people called home was annihilated within ninety seconds.

Elderly Sarah Bean, who had watched a cow float by her window, awoke after briefly losing consciousness to find most of her home gone. Dazed, confused and unable to move or cry loudly for help, Mrs. Bean was pinned under the weight of her life's belongings. Mrs. Bean was alive, however, clinging to life as blood and debris—from where she did not know—pooled on top of her.[32]

Surviving neighbors and other able-bodied men crawled on top of the wreckage in search of the elderly grandparents. She did not know it yet, but her husband of fifty-one years, Harvey; her daughters, Mrs. Ollie Crain and Mrs. Della Cross; her son-in-law Reuben Crain; and her two grandchildren, Opal Rosenberger and Gerald Cross, were all dead, killed from blunt force trauma. A son, two daughters, a brother, a son-in-law and thirteen other grandchildren survived.

Searching through the area, strangers and survivors used doors and sheets of metal as makeshift gurneys to transport Mrs. Bean and dozens of others who had been injured or killed to the basement and first floor of the Gorham School, which, despite having no roof, had more walls left than most other structures in town and gave some protection from the wind and chilling rain.

The makeshift morgue was a gruesome sight. Thirty-seven bodies, including those of several children, were neatly laid out, covered by blankets and sheets. At first, they were solemnly placed in the corner of the Gorham School's basement until space was needed for the living, and they were moved outside. The temperatures dropped. As the evening came, the air chilled to the forties, then the thirties. By nighttime, survivors thought they saw snowflakes, but they were more likely burnt cinders and bits of ashen debris that continued to waft through the sky slowly.

Mrs. Bean arrived at the Gorham School heartbroken, bleeding and in critical condition. Volunteers wrapped her in blankets and comforted her the best anyone knew how while they waited to find a way to transport people out of town. Survivors thought the closest treatment facility was in Murphysboro, twelve miles northeast. But they did not know the tornado that had obliterated their town raced ahead of them and made a direct hit on the region's most populous city.

The closest medical center was now in Cairo, Illinois, over sixty miles and an hour's ride south in the best conditions.

4

JACKSON COUNTY, ILLINOIS

MURPHYSBORO

Murphysboro was the region's largest city, bustling with ten thousand residents, all excited by the economic boom of manufacturing and the thrashing sound of progress from the Mobile and Ohio and Missouri-Pacific Railroads. The railroads converged nearby in a junction of steel rail lines, drawn to the power of the nearby Mississippi and Ohio Rivers.

Manufacturing and commerce had transformed Murphysboro slowly—then quickly. Coal had been discovered near Murphysboro in the bluffs of the Big Muddy River as early as 1800. The Big Muddy Coal and Iron Company was the first coal mine in Illinois, and as soon as it was erected, large flatboats of coal began sailing down the Mississippi River to markets in New Orleans. Despite the closure of the Big Muddy Coal and Iron Company in 1917, the area's reputation changed again when more iron ore operations were started in the late nineteenth century.

For a time, it seemed everyone in Murphysboro was on board for more of everything: jobs, opportunities, money for schools and parks and road and rail connections to bolster the city's industry. Industrial and manufacturing employers took notice and were more than ready to take advantage of the Midwest's lower manufacturing costs.

Among these executives was St. Louis native George Warren Brown, who went to work at his brother's shoe factory in New York in 1873. Almost every kind of shoe in the United States was manufactured on the East Coast and then shipped west to retailers and outlets. But the expense of manufacturing, transporting and retailing these shoes meant most were priced higher than many people in the Midwest and plains could afford.

Brown figured if he could manufacture shoes in St. Louis, he'd have less competition from other shoemakers and lower labor and shipping time costs than anyone else. In 1878, he tested his theory with investors Alvin L. Bryan and Jerome Desnoyers.[33] Together, they founded Bryan, Brown and Company and paid skilled shoemakers from Rochester, New York, to move to St. Louis to manufacture women's shoes. The payoff was immense, with the company's revenue exceeding $100,000 in its first year.

As the investors sold their stakes and retired, Brown renamed the company in 1893 to bear his name: Brown Shoe Company. By 1900, the company was selling over $1 million worth of shoes annually and sold shoes cheaper and faster than its East Coast competitors.

However, these low prices came at a cost, as workers in St. Louis protested the factory's dangerous conditions and the purchase of new machines that relegated shoe manufacturing to a low-skill, low-wage job held mostly by women and children. With this machinery available to competitors, St. Louis was brimming with competing shoe manufacturers that flocked to the area to copy Brown's success.

To keep costs low and avoid labor strife, Brown began operating factories in cheaper areas surrounding St. Louis, starting in Moberly, Missouri, in 1907. Worker frustration resulted in the formation of a union. The first was the moderate Boot and Shoe Workers Union. A more radical United Shoe Workers of America would affiliate itself with the International Workers of the World. Equally frustrated by the workers' demands, Brown left St. Louis.

Brown did not have to look far to find a town willing to put up a factory for the promise of hundreds of new jobs. The arrival of a manufacturer the size of Brown Shoe Company meant more rails, restaurants and retail stores for hundreds of workers. To small-town leaders, that sounded like more of everything when men needed jobs and expected their leaders to deliver.

Cities and towns jumped at any opportunity to take their slice of the nation's immense gains, offering to build factories at no cost to Brown. The incentives continued to escalate just as the company needed them to keep up with demand. There were promises that the company could have a tax-free and subsidized factory that it wouldn't have to pay taxes on for one, two or even three years.

This race to the bottom proved tantalizing when employers could always find another town willing to build and subsidize a factory. By 1910, Brown had grown far enough outside of St. Louis to work with Murphysboro on a new shoe factory that would employ as many as five hundred and produce as many as twenty-two thousand pairs of shoes a week in all styles by 1923. The Murphysboro Brown Shoes plant no. 7 pumped $10,000 of weekly payroll into the local economy.

With rapidly expanding industry, manufacturing and railways, Murphysboro was where Phillip Cline staked his family's name and reputation on a new drugstore. Just as many expected, the boost from major employers proved irresistible to retailers, barbers and professional service workers.

As Cline set up his drugstore, another entrepreneur, Edgar Earl Sims, alongside his son "Ham" Sims, acquired a bakery from J.J. Overly at 1334 Walnut Street. Like the Clines, the Simses felt confident staking their livelihoods on Murphysboro's future. They intended to expand the bakery into a café to feed hundreds of hungry coal, iron and shoe workers and offer refreshing sodas to kids on their way home from school. With the initial sale paperwork completed on March 16, 1925, all the elder Sims needed to do to finalize the transaction was sign the deed and mortgage. Edgar renamed the place Sims Café and worked alongside some of the biggest names in the region.

Late in the morning on March 18, Sims planned to take a train from his home twenty-five miles north in Pinckneyville to finalize the sale. Stepping out on his front porch amid gusty winds, he sensed something was off. It was only drizzling, but something about the thick clouds wafting overhead persuaded him to go back inside. He would buy his diner later.

The nuns at St. Anders Catholic School, the oldest school in Murphysboro, also felt something unusual. They couldn't see anything but heard thunder and lightning around 2:30 p.m. As the winds increased and daylight decreased, the nuns ushered the students into the basement and instructed them all to pray as they ran.

At the nearby Logan School, built in 1884 as the first school in town, students and teachers ran into the corner of their classrooms.[34] Young boys and girls huddled on the floor as far away from the windows as possible, protected by a meager table or desk. The two-story brick building featured grand windows nearly as tall as the building itself, designed to let light stream in on the desks and minds of students.

The light that had streamed in under diffuse white clouds dwindled, like a light bulb being slowly covered by a sheet. A monstrous clap of thunder shook the earth. Students gazed over their shoulders and saw a vile green-black hue glowing through the windows. Many more began to pray.

Students and teachers in the front yard of the Logan School sometime before the storm. *Sallie Logan Public Library*.

Young Mary Belle Melvin, who was sheltering in the corner of her classroom with her classmates, looked up long enough to see a photograph of a young boy holding a rabbit clamber against the wall. Distressed the glass might break, her teacher asked one of Mary Belle's classmates to take it down.

The tornado that had swept away Gorham minutes earlier was now ninety minutes old and bearing down on Murphysboro. At the end of town, the top of one house was peeled off and carried away. The first floor remained intact, and the second story's floor now formed the structure's roof. A bed on the second floor was scarcely tousled.[35] The bell tower on top of city hall came crashing down with a sickening thud near the Rathgeber store. Business owners and customers downtown raced for vaults, back rooms, safes, freezers and anything that looked bolted down.

Huddling in the corner of their classrooms, students at the Logan School could hear the storm's mighty gusts. The windows seemed to bow and ache under the intense pressure until every window blew in violently, shattering into hundreds of pieces of shrapnel and whipping papers, books, globes and other supplies into a lethal frenzy.

Across the street from the Logan School, a local grocer pulled up in his Model T Ford as the sky quickly darkened. He ran inside the market just in time to witness his beautiful new car move backward, almost as if in reverse, until it was flattened by a felled telephone pole.

Four-year-old Bertha Seltser was sitting in her kindergarten classroom on the first floor of another school in town.[36] The Longfellow School, a grand three-story brick building erected at the start of the century, sat on the edge of town. Fearing the storm was moving quicker than the students could run, teachers hurriedly ushered everyone into the basement. Bertha and a neighborhood boy who lived two blocks away were too afraid of the darkening skies to stay in the building. Instead of ducking into the basement like everyone else, they darted upstairs for home.

Just as the two children opened the door to look outside, the mile-wide cyclone bore down on the building, its thick clouds ripping bricks away from the mortar. A large portion of the roof was torn back like a lid, but what remained hanging onto the Longfellow School's frame collapsed inward. Without structural support, the remains of the brick walls buckled inward, crushing the students and teachers who were sheltering in the basement.

The force of the wind knocked Bertha and the other young boy back into the hallway, but the debris miraculously managed to make only a small cut across Bertha's head.

"Baldy" Fisher, as he was known around town, was working outside at the Mobile and Ohio Railroad yard.[37] A machinist responsible for keeping the train engines working, he was staring at the torn-apart skeleton of a mammoth train engine when the tornado's relentless wind emanated through the railyard. As Baldy was no stranger to the sound of locomotives and freight cars, he missed the warning signs as the tornado's immense cloud bore down on him. Seeking shelter, Fisher frantically crawled into an empty two-by-four-foot piston cylinder tube mounted inside a locomotive engine. The cylinder was just large enough for a man to fit inside, so Baldy curled up into the chamber as its walls echoed with the pings of rain, hail and debris. Inside the fifty-ton engine car, the raindrops sounded like bullets, and the hail and debris sounded like cannonballs. The train engine rocked back and forth in the wind for three minutes as heavy debris forced some parts of the shop walls to cave in from direct strikes. "It rocked like a cradle," he said afterward. "I was afraid every minute the locomotive would go over."

Inside the shop buildings, men dove under heavy steel workbenches, cars and anything else that seemed big enough for a man to fit in or under. Peeking out from under the benches, these men saw the wind lift great sections of brick walls and send them sailing away as if they were bedsheets. Men hollered and yelled for their friends and coworkers to take cover.

The devastation surrounding the Longfellow School in Murphysboro, Illinois. *Jackson County, Illinois Historical Society collections.*

Reminiscent of soldiers in a foxhole helplessly peering out at no-man's-land, they watched as their friends and colleagues were struck or impaled by loose timber, steel and brick.

The walls that were not cleanly lifted away collapsed on people's heads and makeshift shelters. Men prayed first for themselves and their families and then for the men next to them. Amid the tangle of steel and brick, dozens of men were smothered to death. Large furnaces that had been at work minutes earlier, heating tools and powering equipment, toppled over, sending tons of burning coals and embers out onto the shop floor and around the yard. For the men who avoided being crushed to death, the noxious fumes propelled by fire suffocated them under rubble.

The worst fate was reserved for those who had not yet been crushed or suffocated—they could sense the nearing heat of the spreading fire. They could only yell from under the debris as powerless men feet above them had no way to extinguish the fires or dig out their friends. The stifling mortar and brick would become their deathbed.

Others, like "Buster" Brown, had just left the area next to a water cooler when the storm sent walls, roofing and mortar sailing. No trace of him was ever found. Sheets of walls and signage, including a five-by-six-foot iron sheet, whisked through the air and into the side of Frank Henson's home at Twentieth and Clark Streets, nearly two miles away. Six men carried the sheet out of the remnants of the home several hours after the storm. Crawling out from under the remnants of their workplace, most men wondered how anyone could have been lucky enough to survive. "Baldy" Fisher, who had crawled inside the piston cylinder, unfurled himself, totally unharmed.

Within three minutes, 234 people had died in Murphysboro, the most deaths in a single tornado in any community in U.S. history. Half of the survivors were left homeless, as 150 blocks had been completely smeared across the earth. "Hours of battering by field artillery could do no more to a town than the tornado did to the stricken area of Murphysboro," wrote one reporter for the *McHenry Plaindealer* just after the storm. "Brick buildings went with the weaker frames. Thirty-seven children were crushed to death in the collapse of two school buildings. Two square miles with 500 residences and 100 businesses were leveled."[38]

Five hundred workers at the Mobile and Ohio railyard were trapped when the roof of the depot and railyards collapsed. Thirty-five men were killed, and hundreds more were seriously injured. Those who escaped the wreckage stood torn between their duty to the men beside them and their families blocks away. Hundreds of parents raced to the Longfellow, Logan and St. Andrews Schools in search of their children. The Lincoln School and the segregated Washington School were spared the heaviest damage.

The damage at the once-massive Missouri-Pacific Railroad shops in Murphysboro, Illinois. *Jackson County, Illinois Historical Society collections.*

The Lincoln School after the storm in Murphysboro, Illinois. *Sallie Logan Public Library.*

A ten-year-old boy who clambered out of the Logan School ran into town, shouting, "The school fell on the children, the Logan School!" Survivors raced through mangled streets toward the school. Rounding the corner, they found a stream of schoolchildren frantically crying and running in all directions. Rescuers clawed at the debris with nothing but their bare hands and adrenaline. Frantically calling out names above the cries and shrieks of terrified adolescents, parents faced the grim reality that eleven students were dead.

The eastern half of the Logan School located under the stairs held up during the storm, and most students under the stairs survived with only scrapes and cuts. The men who were digging for children under the second-story walls lifted survivors out and passed them along like water in a bucket brigade. Then they started pulling out dead children—two, three, four, five. Chief of Police Joe Boston found his daughter's body in the ruins. Reverend Abbott and his wife found their son, Thomas, hanging in a tree. The tornado had picked him up and blown him into a battered tree, where he remained clinging for dear life, uninjured. A stranger picked up Bertha Seltser, who had attempted to race up and out of the school to get home, only to be blown down the stairs. Frightened but alive, she was placed on the ground outside the wreckage. Someone placed a rug over her to keep her warm. The boy who had run beside her did not survive.

Left: Women watch as men in the background dig through the rubble for the bodies of schoolchildren killed at the Logan School in Murphysboro. *Jackson County, Illinois Historical Society collections.*

Below: The total collapse of the Logan School in Murphysboro, Illinois. *Sallie Logan Public Library.*

The rain continued to fall lightly as the skies gradually showed signs it was still daylight. A short while later, a stranger led Seltser to the basement of a blown-away house. Her grandparents found her four hours later, around 7:00 p.m. She looked on as men continued to sift through the school's remains. Standing on top of the debris pile that stretched a story and a half into the air, men could see the remains of Murphysboro and the fires lashing out all around them.

After the tornado passed, teachers at the Logan, Longfellow and St. Andrews Schools and the high school faced a choice about what to do with the children in their care. All the buildings had been struck, splintering the structures and their support beams and sending mud, dirt and grime into the faces and bodies of everyone inside. Some were bruised, but most were able to walk. Nine were dead at the Longfellow School, and three were dead at the high school.[39]

Everyone at St. Andrews walked away from the storm. About two dozen students and teachers there had scratches from the blown-in window glass and other lacerations to their faces or hands. Arquilla Wade, one of the few Black students there, suffered burns to her hands, presumably from a toppled furnace.[40] Still, the nuns refused to allow anyone to leave. Crawling

Top: A panorama view of Twenty-First Street in Murphysboro after the storm. The Longfellow School can be seen in the center. *Sallie Logan Public Library*.

Bottom: A panorama view of the area surrounding the Logan School in Murphysboro, Illinois. *Sallie Logan Public Library*.

out from the basement, sometimes over rafters and beams, no one knew what God had wrought across town, but it was instantly recognizable that wires were down everywhere, cars were bent around stumps of once-grand one-hundred-year-old trees and countless people were feared injured or dead. The safest place, the nuns decided, was right where they were, if for no other reason than surviving parents would know where to find their students.

At the Logan School, so little of the building was left that it was decided the kids were better off finding their way back to whatever was left of their homes. In the schoolyard, students filed by a one-by-ten-foot board that had been driven into a tree. It was so firmly ensconced in the tree that kids and men who weighed up to 150 pounds could put all their weight on it without it so much as wiggling. The tree was removed a few days later and put on display in the statehouse in Springfield.[41]

The roof of the Brown Shoe Company, which was torn off by the storm. *Sallie Logan Public Library*.

Students were told to watch out for wires, nails, glass and other debris as they walked off in a daze. The force of the mud and grime pummeled against their bodies tore off their clothes and rendered their skin and faces nearly unrecognizable. At first, students wondered if their classmates were of another species. Some students suffered bruising; others had minor cuts and lacerations that sent blood streaming down their faces, arms and legs, only to dry against the black mud splattered across their bodies.

Most parents and workers at the nearby Brown Shoe Company faced little issue getting out from under debris, since most of the building and the entire top floor of the formerly three-story building was neatly shorn off and blown to the side like the top blanket of a bed. But a portion of the third floor had collapsed in on workmen.

The tornado passed over Murphysboro at sixty miles per hour. Many residents described it simply, "It was dark, it was windy, then it was over." Some described it as "three big gusts," a sensation that was unheard of and never experienced in any storm anyone could remember. The north side of Murphysboro was a solid mass of splintered, shattered homes and lives. Yet amid brief torrents of rain, the dark storm clouds moved on, and it seemed to turn brighter at around 3:00 p.m.

In three minutes, the tornado marched across Murphysboro. The devastation to life and property in the town elevated the storm to historic new levels. Unlike the towns of Gorham or Annapolis, which had large

Top: A residential area of Murphysboro destroyed by the storm. *Jackson County, Illinois Historical Society collections.*

Bottom: A residential area of Murphysboro after the storm. *Jackson County, Illinois Historical Society collections.*

hills, hollows and rock formations along or near one side or another, Murphysboro sat at the junction of a new landscape, one unencumbered by natural barriers and protections. Only the Big Muddy River presented itself as an insignificant and powerless barrier. Yet to most locals, it was believed Murphysboro sat in a near-mythical "hole," and no serious storm could threaten them. This myth was shattered in about 180 seconds.

AFTER TORNADO AND FIRE MURPHYSBORO ILL. WE

Wandering out of the hole that was once the Logan School, students bore witness to their town's devastation. Detached limbs hung in the scant few branches left in the trees. Legs and feet, sometimes with shoes still on, and hands reaching out were visible under collapsed roofs, walls and large trees. Roosters evolved to loosen their feathers for a quick escape from a predator's jaws. Now, in a state of shock, they clucked along the streets stripped bare, without a single feather on their bodies. One woman was found unharmed; she had taken cover in her bathtub, only to have the tub be flung into the air and become lodged in a now largely limbless tree. Compared to most buildings, the Lincoln, Washington and Douglass Schools suffered significant damage and were left without roofs and walls. But they could be repaired. The new $267,000 addition to the high school was demolished. St. Andrews School was partly unroofed.

In the immediate aftermath, fire seemingly threatened more lives than the tornado. Flames lashed the sky and leaped out of the wreckage of the Mobile and Ohio railyard, where shifting winds fueled fires from overturned stoves, furnaces and fireplaces, sending fiery tongues of heat through the wrecked city. Half an hour after the storm, flames stretched from Walnut Street through the levee and across a mile and a half of streets in an unbroken firewall.

Anything that had not been fully destroyed by the wind in the business district came under threat of burning. Those who had survived the tornado now had to avoid being burned alive as flames devoured the debris around them. In a dark twist of the storm's winds, people whose entire homes or businesses had been swept cleanly from their foundations found themselves in better safety from fire than those whose properties had collapsed on top of them like kindling.

A panorama view of Murphysboro from an unknown location. *Sallie Logan Public Library.*

Attempting to get ahead of the fire proved challenging for fire crews, as water pressure failed at fire hydrants across town. The new powerhouse, which supplied electricity to the water pumps, had collapsed in, releasing steam into the air. Injured, afraid and unaware of their own families' plights, powerhouse workmen valiantly restored water service within two hours by manually pumping water into the underground mains directly from the Big Muddy River.

Over the next several hours, the combined forces from seven fire companies from Cairo, Murphysboro, Carbondale, Anna, Zeigler, Benton and Herrin, Illinois, crawled through the streets in an unrivaled effort to extinguish the fires armed with a seemingly endless supply of water from the river. Undeterred, the fires moved so quickly that a new $12,000 fire truck from the Herrin Fire Department raced into Murphysboro alongside other companies, only to become mired in the mud of a back alley and burned up on its inaugural run.[42]

Teams of men rushed to strategic areas like Sixteenth and Walnut Streets to search for survivors before the fire arrived. A woman who was stuck but alive under the weight of her home at Twenty-First and Hortense Streets had her legs amputated by an overwhelmed doctor who had no choice but to revert to nineteenth-century medicine, mostly carrying out amputations with better antiseptic and no anesthetic. It was the only way to free the woman before the flames arrived. Fire companies armed whatever capable men they could find with dynamite to blow up entire city blocks, hoping to reduce the fire's fuel.

The ghastly reality, though, was evident, as the risk of dynamiting potential survivors or the bodies of their neighbors chilled everyone who

Top: Mobile and Ohio Railroad shops in Murphysboro, Illinois. *Sallie Logan Public Library*.

Bottom: Fires rage through homes and businesses along Spruce Street in Murphysboro just after the storm. *Sallie Logan Public Library*.

Opposite: Residents scramble around the fires torching Seventeenth Street in Murphysboro shortly after the storm. *Sallie Logan Public Library*.

placed the explosives. The plan seemed to work until the fire blew across an alley near Tippey's restaurant and began spreading again, sending ribbons of smoke into the air. Despite the town's men exploding hundreds of pounds of dynamite, there was too much fuel scattered around. The dynamite merely shuffled the wreckage from one pile to another smaller pile. The fire carried on.

Everyone thought the entire town was likely to go up in flames. The new $85,000 Baptist church, which was set to be formally opened that Sunday, was reduced to tinder. A funeral was being held there when the tornado struck. Staff and guests huddled in the basement at the Blue Front Hotel as the tornado's fierce winds blew overhead. Against nearly three-hundred-mile-per-hour winds, eighteen people survived. But their basement refuge from the storm became a trap, and all eighteen burned to death. The men who working above could do nothing but listen to the agonizing screams and pangs of terror of those trapped below. No amount of hand tools or manpower could move that much rubble quickly, and no amount of time could pass to erase the memory of the shrieks that emanated from below until the fire burned its captives to death.

Residents who survived the tornado, the fires and the immediate shock still had to contend with the fourth horseman of the calamity: disease. Debris snarled into precarious positions at every step. Dozens in Murphysboro died from infections after suffering scrapes and cuts and stepping on nails. Dozens more lost limbs from infection. Ambulances, trucks and men carrying people in their arms raced amid the rattle of ambulance bells and horns, immediately maxing out the capacity of the hospital. Makeshift hospitals

The charred remains of the Blue Front Hotel in Murphysboro after fires swept the city. Eighteen people died after being trapped in the fire. *Sallie Logan Public Library*.

were established at the Presbyterian church, the Odd Fellows lodge and anywhere else that had some semblance of structure.

The dead quickly overwhelmed the morgue. Stecker's Brewery, with its now vast and empty basement, was mostly spared from the storm. But it wasn't spared from Prohibition, which had shuttered the bottling plant five years earlier. For now, it found new use as a makeshift morgue. Disease from the dead and cooling temperatures, along with scarlet fever and tetanus, began to pose a silent but no less deadly threat to the survivors of the tornado and its fiery aftermath.

A long, cold night would pass before the rest of the world heard about the storm and could rush in to help. Those who slept outside could sense the temperatures sinking to about forty degrees. The wind shifted from a warm southeasterly breeze to a brisk northern wind. Each stiff gust felt like scouring ice as men righted barrels and stoves to light fires and huddled their families together in overturned railcars, empty basements or the remains of houses on the other side of town. Alas, the fires those men had fought against for hours began running out of fuel past 2:00 or 3:00 a.m., sinking thousands into chilly darkness and forcing everyone to retreat to the muted dusk of grief.

5
DE SOTO, ILLINOIS

"IT SEEMS THAT I AM THE ONLY PERSON ALIVE."

Students at the De Soto School in Illinois began whispering to each other as they looked out their classroom windows, wondering if the sky was prophesizing. As they peeked out, it seemed the sky was engaged in battle. Students whispered along, "A storm's coming up." Despite their teacher's best effort to keep them on their lessons, the more the kids whispered to each, the more they craned their necks and adjusted their posture from behind wooden desks and chairs to get a better look. The children could see much of De Soto from their vantage point at the school.

The De Soto School was three stories tall, counting a basement. The school's sharp roof formed distinct angles over neatly arranged windows that were as tall as each floor. Grade schoolers attended classes on the first floor, and high school students heard lessons on the second floor. The school's sturdy brick masonry was a point of pride in town, as there was no end to the bricks in a city where nearly everything was built of brick, thanks to the local brickworks.

Five hundred people called De Soto home. Life there was challenging, but electricity had just been wired into the village over the last few years, making living easier. Not since 1854, when the first railroad extended into the new village, had things felt so futuristic and comfortable in De Soto. There were a few hundred homes and dozens of shops, feed stores and a few small mining operations in town. Shops, restaurants and bakeries offered endless goods and confections. Most people who lived in De Soto couldn't have imagined anything like it just a generation prior. Everything from fried chicken to meatloaf, doughnuts and bread was made fresh daily.

A photograph of the De Soto School with students and educators out front taken some time before the storm. *Sallie Logan Public Library.*

Sitting near the middle of town around 2:30 p.m. was the large red brick home of George Albon. Born in Canada in 1858, the thin, wiry man of sixty-seven was often seen walking and driving around town in his neatly tailored suits and ties with his wife, Abbie May.[43] Albon was a partner of Walker and Albon, general merchandisers. His father, James, had come to the United States in 1860 and operated the De Soto Mill off and on for many years.

George set off to make his own way in dry goods and sales at the age of fifteen, and this job had made him a wealthy man by 1925. His first wife, Blanche Friedline, died in March 1889, leaving behind a sole surviving daughter, Lucille. George met Abbie Walker a year later and soon had two more children, George Jr. and Arthur. A devout Lutheran and Democrat, George was well-liked in De Soto.[44] Neighbors could count on his support for politics, the school and the general welfare of the small village.

Nearby, Gertrude Bullar and her young daughter, Lala, were in their craftsman home tending to the newest member of the Bullar family, baby Ruth. Her sons Andrew and Carl were at the De Soto School, no doubt anxiously watching the clock for recess. Gertrude and the family were cut from hearty midwestern stock. Back in January, Bullar's father, Andrew Graeff, died at the age of eighty. He was the last living soldier from Jackson County who had marched in Civil War general William Tecumseh Sherman's famous March to the Sea in late 1864.[45]

Fourteen-year-old Garret Crews was also in school that day, watching the clock tick down. Crews was a familiar site before and after school each day as he walked along or near the Illinois Central Railroad, about three blocks away, to a two-story building that marked the northern point of the De Soto business district, his home.

At precisely 2:36 p.m., gusts of strong wind came howling overhead. They surely would have struck Gertrude Bullar's father as loud and raucous as any battle of the Civil War. A brow of fog hung over the horizon, spilling rain and debris. Almost no one saw it coming. John Cummings and his family were in their home when the storm struck at a furious speed. They felt the house rise from its foundations, twirl completely around and settle down to the ground about fifteen yards from its former site. The house was not damaged, nor was the family.

Jackson County sheriff's deputy George Boland was on patrol just outside of town that afternoon.[46] Noticing the thickening clouds ahead of him, Deputy Boland probably thought it was a dust storm. Whatever it was, he saw it fit to step out of his patrol car and walk into the middle of the road for a better look. Peering up, Deputy Boland confused the mammoth mile-wide tornado for a strange cloud, because it did not appear to be moving. (When a tornado appears as if it's not moving, only growing larger, it is coming straight at you.) With each sporadic lightning bolt, the funnel cloud illuminated itself, appearing larger than it had been the flash before. Witnesses who looked out their windows said the deputy was picked up fifty feet in the air and carried east over the railroad tracks with a torrent of debris. His body was never found.

Jesse Pankey drove his car into a garage when he felt the wind picking up. As he exited the automobile, it rose through the garage roof and disappeared, carrying his wife and children with it. The prankish wind whisked him five blocks away before setting him down, unhurt. His wife and children were later found in a freshly plowed field, only slightly harmed and more than a little frightened.[47]

Frank Hewitt, a former Illinois State senator and longtime druggist in Carbondale, was visiting a friend in De Soto when he saw the immense gray and black cloud approaching on the horizon. "It was cleaning the surface of the Earth as it came. Like a huge plane," he said.

"I went with Thomas Cherry," he told a reporter later, "to the home of a De Soto woman to transact some business. The lady was showing us her six-week-old twins when we saw the clouds looming on the horizon."

Hewitt, Cherry and the woman stepped outside to get a better look at the big, boiling clouds looming over the horizon. "I believe it's a tornado!" cried Hewitt.

Scooping up the newborn twins, the trio ran across the street to another woman, who was also carrying a baby, to watch the phenomenon. Now, all four adults and their three children could see the storm coming nearer amid intermittent flashes of lightning. Timber and other debris appeared to be floating in the air along the wind's crest.

"Let's go inside," one of the women remarked.

"No, we should stay here," said Hewitt, perhaps on the assumption they could move out of its way. Realizing everyone around him was darting inside, he relented, and everyone crowded into the neighbor's home.

Within seconds, "the wind increased to the roar of a tremendous draft when it sounded like a lumbering wagon coming down the street," recalled Hewitt. "Suddenly, the house we were in was lifted about ten feet and moved through the air. Settling about twenty feet distant."

Figuring they were surely safer outside than they were inside, the entire household exited the home as fast as they could. Running into the mighty winds, Mr. Cherry was immediately knocked unconscious by flying timber and the tumbling contents of hundreds of other homes and businesses.

"I felt like I was going to fly, and was being drawn straight up into the air, then I fell down," Hewitt recalled. "I saw a post nearby and thought if I could get to it, I would not be sucked into the air," Hewitt said. Crawling along the ground, his body aching from the timber strike and unable to see more than a few dozen feet ahead, Hewitt reached the post and held tight.

Ever the politician, Hewitt told a reporter later, "I felt rather foolish and wondered what people would think if they saw me lying flat on the ground and holding fast to a fence post....As we came from the house, we could see houses and other buildings lifted into the air in a mass, and then could see them disintegrating." Most buildings are capable of withstanding even relatively strong straight-line winds head on. But the pressure differential within a tornado's funnel lifts and twists buildings like a top, disintegrating them as they pass through. Combined with other debris that is being turned into two- or three-hundred-mile-per-hour battering rams, few structures can withstand the fury.

The general view of De Soto, Illinois, after the storm. *Sallie Logan Public Library.*

Just as quickly as it began, the rushing wagon train of wind was over. Peering up, Hewitt looked down at himself, dirty and soaked in muddy water. An intense ringing in his head momentarily confused him until a surge of adrenaline washed it away amid the cries of babies everywhere. Frantic mothers searched for children who had been ripped from their arms, calling out names and screaming at the top of their lungs.

"I got to my feet and looked around. It seemed to me that bodies were everywhere, particularly the bodies of old people and of children. Some of them were red with blood, and some of them had all their clothing torn off," recalled Hewitt.

"I tried to help the women hunting for their children. Then I heard the screaming of the injured. I would go to one person, and start elsewhere to get help for him, only to find another person more desperately hurt. Then I would hear another cry and find another still more seriously injured. I never turned to the same person twice."

Gazing around the foggy aftermath, Hewitt muttered, "It seems that I am the only person alive." Short of breath and suffering from intense panic and stress, he realized he had survived the tornado's initial onslaught but began to wonder if he might suffocate instead. A neighbor a short distance away began to stir and move around from behind a pile of debris. "It seemed to me he and I were the only persons left, and I felt that he was the only friend I had in the world and didn't want to lose sight of him," Hewitt recounted.[48]

Together, the two new friends pulled out the dead and injured from the wrecked homes surrounding them until others came out to help. Looking around, Hewitt discovered all the women and their children nearest him had escaped the storm and were mostly unhurt.

Back at the De Soto School, a group of boys and seven-year-old Betty Barnett Moroni kept tossing hats in the air to see how far the wind might blow them. It seemed that each time they chased after their hats and threw them in the air, the wind carried them farther and farther. Inside, the school's janitor, Gilbert Williams, whom the students called "Uncle Gill," saw the blinds flapping erratically in the windows. Sensing a storm might be coming up, he rang the bell to get students in from afternoon recess.

After lining up and filing into the building, Garrett Crews, Andrew and Carl Bullar and their classmates moved upstairs to their classrooms. The incoming rain had lightly soaked the shoulders and hair of many students. The blinds were flapping erratically at the open windows as they paced into their classrooms, slightly out of breath. The teachers enjoyed the breeze until the rain started to blow in. "Will the boys please run over and close the windows and blinds?" the teachers asked. The boys in each classroom ran over to close them. Moroni took her seat next to her sister, ten-year-old Marie.

Looking up as they reached for the windows, the boys all paused. The young men on the southwest corner of the building saw the sky filled with thousands of bits of sheet metal, trees, wood and other debris. Across the entire school building, the boys reached the windows as clouds darkened their rooms. Eager to get started with their final lesson of the day, teachers encouraged the boys to hurry up and return to their seats. Transfixed by what they saw, the boys remained by the windows.

Garrett Crews looked down from an upstairs classroom long enough to see two wooden basketball goalposts vibrating back and forth until they finally snapped and flew off into the air. The force of the wind pummeled glass and metal into the side of the building like spears, shattering windows and immediately killing nearly all the young boys who had rushed over to close the windows. Only three boys in Betty Moroni's class survived.

Students on all floors screamed and cried out in unified terror as the windows shattered inward and parts of the roof began to break away. Downstairs, Gertrude Bullar's two boys, Andrew and Carl, aged fourteen and nine, respectively, looked up at the ceiling as bricks and mortar rained down. The school's second floor was ripped away from the first floor like a tin lid. Anything that wasn't immediately blown away began to collapse in on the first floor and basement.

Already six feet tall and as strong as any of his classmates, Garrett Crews struggled to move against the force of the wind. He couldn't see his desk or classmates anymore or make out what was happening outside. Removed of its upper floors and lacking a frame support, the school's first and second floors began to dissolve along with the walls. Students collapsed with the floors as they frantically pushed into the hallways and stairwells, ultimately piling together in a mass of desks, chairs and bodies somewhere between the basement and first floor. Since the storm was moving at fifty-six miles per hour and reaching sustained winds of sixty miles per hour, no one could hear their screams over the force of relentless sheets of rain and ceaseless wind.

Landing on top of someone who was bleeding, Crews, awake and conscious, looked up long enough to grab hold of a doorframe and catch sight of one of three girls standing near the outdoor toilet. Nearly locking eyes with the girl, Crews clung to the frame as the wind lifted her a few feet off the ground and blew her "more or less straight north," he recalled, like she was pulled by a dozen wild horses. Crews closed his eyes and began to pray.[49]

So much was gone. Gone were the school's sturdy bricks, left in a helpless pile. Gone were the town's shops and confectioneries, craftsmen's homes and mighty oak and maple trees outside. After waking up and regaining his bearings, Andrew Bullar began to dig his way up through his school's wreckage. The only thing left standing was the front façade and a few layers of bricks that once marked the start of the first-floor foundation. Surfacing within a couple

The littered remains of the De Soto, Illinois School. *Jackson County, Illinois Historical Society collections.*

of feet, the yells of children's names filled the air, pierced by the screams of people who were waking up and noticing that death surrounded them. Andrew had seen his brother Carl nearby in the hallway when the storm hit and began digging for him through the rubble. Help wasn't far away, but no one in town was aware of the extent of what had just happened to their sleepy village.

"Carl!" Andrew yelled, hoping anyone might point out where his brother was. Picking through, he found his younger brother under a shallow layer of bricks and debris. Carl's eye socket was cut in a line straight down to his jaw, leaving his eye bulging out and bleeding. Scooping Carl up, Andrew ran across town to the home of George Albon—the only house still standing. No one was inside, but he found a blanket and wrapped his brother up before he ran home to check on his sisters Ruth and Lala and their mother, Gertrude.

After reciting his prayers, Garrett Crews opened his eyes and looked down his leg to find blood on his pants and shoes. He did not feel terribly hurt but was pinned between a beam and Uncle Gil, the janitor. "Don't worry, son," Uncle Gill called down to Crews. "If I can just move some bricks under me, that'll free you." Crews soon realized he did not feel pain because he had not suffered a scratch. The blood trickling down his leg was from Uncle Gil, who was bald and bleeding from his exposed scalp.

With a free arm to remove some bricks and debris, Uncle Gil twisted himself free enough to loosen the tension on Crews. Young, shocked and completely unaware of what to do about the nightmare unfolding before him, Crews ran for home, passing the body of the girl he had seen blown out of the toilet now caught dead in a fence. Years later, Crews regretted fleeing in such terror.

Betty Moroni was trapped under debris but survived by crawling out and over the rubble. Moroni's sister and nineteen of her classmates had died almost instantly. Moroni lost three sisters, and her father later died of head injuries he sustained during the tornado.

"After the tornado was over, nobody knew where anybody was," she told the *Southern Illinoisian* in 2015. Looking around, she did not recognize anything or know where she was. The town was gone.[50]

Running for his life, Garrett Crews took his usual way back toward what was the train depot and the two-story general store and Oddfellows lodge that marked the northern end of De Soto's business district. Men yelled at Crews to watch for wires as he raced as fast as his lungs would carry him. The new electrical wires were strewn across the street. Able-bodied men—and some who were not— tried directing people out of their homes and businesses and away from downed power lines.

Fire was everywhere, including at the two-story Oddfellows lodge that marked Crews's turn toward school and home. The fire was so hot and suffocating that he couldn't pass it. Turning back for a new path, he found the sidewalks covered with glass and nails. Running on sheer adrenaline, he sprinted back a few blocks before finding another way north. Sensing he was about halfway to where he thought his home used to be, he came across a man holding an infant in the street, presumably just in front of what was the man's house. The father, moved to tears, held his dead child in his arms.

Crews stepped directly onto a nail that was protruding from a piece of split lumber in his haste to get home. So much debris covered the roads, sidewalks and yards, it was hard to step anywhere else. The nail pierced the sole of Crews's sneaker and the ball of his foot, exposing him to tetanus. Since Crews was still in shock, the pain was intense but not debilitating. Placing his other foot on the board, Crews seethed as he lifted his injured foot and shoe off the nail. Still hurrying to get home, he took off again to where he used to live—the first house on the first street in the southwest corner of town. There was no house anywhere to be seen or any indication that any house had ever been there.

Andrew Bullar reached his mother and sister Lala after leaving his brother in a blanket at the Albon house in the middle of town. Out of breath, Andrew found his mother's arms covered in blood. Lala was still searching for the newborn Ruth but couldn't find the courage to venture far from her mother.

Gertrude Bullar's home and 30 percent of the rest of De Soto had been destroyed in under ninety seconds as the twister continued its forward march across Illinois. After being knocked in the head with debris, Gertrude woke up sometime after the storm passed to find she had been blown out the front door and into the street; she was now lying under a tree, bleeding severely from her arms.

Her daughter Lala had been blown into a nearby tree that had miraculously clung to the earth. Lala was holding her baby sister Ruth but lost sight after a brief bit of unconsciousness. Lala awoke and looked down from the tree to see her mother. Lala tried to cry out. She had been hit in the head either by debris or the tree she had been blown into, and nerve damage rendered her face akin to that of a stroke victim. One eyelid drooped. Her hands were burned, most likely from a hot stove she had clung to before the home was fully torn asunder.

Clambering down from the tree, Lala came to her mother's side. With the calmness only a mother could bring to such a situation, Gertrude patiently and calmly told Lala, "Honey, you've gotta cord my arms or I'm gonna bleed to death."

Looking around for fabric or cloth to tie off her mother's arms, Lala ripped apart a blanket. "Honey, don't tie too tight; it'll stop the circulation," said Gertrude, pointing midway between her elbow and forearm. Lala's hands and clothes were covered in her mother's blood, which had been gushing until she tied with enough pressure to stop it. Just then, Andrew rushed up, gasping for breath.

"How's Carl?" Gertrude asked, realizing only one of her sons was there with her.

"He's OK," Andrew lied. At the tender age of fourteen, Andrew recognized his brother was likely dead or nearly so, his baby sister was missing and his mother was gravely injured.

Everyone across De Soto ran in all directions to search for loved ones and any supplies that might be able to render care. A bystander near Gertrude and Lala found an infant in the street—baby Ruth. They placed the infant in a potato bin, either unsure of how to provide more care or in a hurry to help someone in worse condition. Burned but seemingly calm, Lala found baby Ruth nearby and rushed back to her mother.

In dire need of a hospital, Andrew ran up and down the street. He eventually found a group of four men who were digging through the rubble of a home, searching for a deceased woman. "My mother's alive, and she needs help," Andrew yelled, his heart beating intensely. "Will you see that she gets to the hard road and to the hospital? We can get the dead later," he said, with stunning clarity and prescience for a fourteen-year-old.

Rushing back with Andrew, the four men found a blanket and hoisted Gertrude onto a mattress. They carried her to a road where a vegetable truck was waiting to go to DuQuoin and the nearest hospital. Lala loaded up alongside her mother. "I have to go back for Carl," Andrew said as the truck prepared to drive off.

Andrew ran back to his baby sister with the hope that another car would come by. A car being driven by Harold Lancaster and his wife came up just in time to find Andrew and the baby, who were so thoroughly caked in black soot, debris and mud, the couple thought they were Black children. "We have to get my brother," Andrew said to the driver, pointing toward the Albon house.

The trio and baby Ruth drove to the house standing in the middle of town, which had become a makeshift triage center. Andrew picked up Carl, who was still alive but in intense pain from his eye injury. "We'll drive him to the hospital in DuQuoin," Mr. Lancaster told him, "But first, you and your sister can stay at my house," he said, driving up to the damaged but standing stately home. The generous benefactor told Andrew, "My personal nurse will look after the baby and help you get cleaned up." Driving off with the injured Bullar, the Lancasters arrived in DuQuoin in time for the doctors to preserve Carl's eye. Carl Bullar later served in World War II. He died in 1984 at the age of sixty-eight.

Outside of town, immediately following the storm, Illinois Central Railroad telegraph operator Max Burton heard about De Soto's condition and rushed in from his Tamaroa, Illinois office to help.[51] Rail traffic south and west of the tornado began to catch up with Burton and the twister. He was only two and a half miles north of the De Soto School and was among the first outsiders to come into town to bear witness to the devastated school.

Gasping for air after rushing to the town, Burton's breath was taken away again as he looked around the day's remains. A few adults had come to the school to help. "Rescue workers were piling the little bodies of the children on mattresses and blankets on the playground, outside of the schoolhouse," he recalled. "It seems there was no one there to claim them. Their parents were being taken to hospitals on special trains and ambulances." Twenty tender-age bodies lined the playground, where they had played mere hours earlier. The few rescuers who were available scratched their way, brick by brick, until they could identify a hand, a shoe or a face. So many were bruised and blackened by the storm, their flesh blended in with the bricks like camouflage.

"A few yards beyond the schoolhouse, in a field near the city limits, I saw the bodies of two little babies about six or eight months old," Burton recalled. "Both were dead. Their clothes were torn, and they had apparently been blown there by the fierce wind." So many infants and small children had been blown so far away from their families that it took days for them to be positively identified. "The principal of the school was on hand," said Burton. "He was trying to identify the bodies of the pupils, also worrying over the whereabouts and safety of two girl teachers who were unaccounted for." The principal stood bloodied, staggering with each step and flush with panic and adrenaline.

Powerless to protect the students and teachers at the school, the rescuers and principal felt heat mounting underfoot. A fire in the De Soto School's furnace was moving through the wreckage like lightning, sending smoke up through the debris in search of the surface. The fire breathed in fresh oxygen from the remaining wind gusts. As the fire was sheltered by the debris, the

Residents inspect and grieve at the site of the De Soto, Illinois School. *Sallie Logan Public Library.*

last remaining raindrops wrung from the clouds were powerless to stem its insatiable demand for fuel. Overpowered and outmanned, the few available rescuers on site retreated off the smoldering rubble. Whatever the tornado had not destroyed, the fire would now incinerate. Anyone who was not already out of the school was trapped.

Turning away from the grisly blaze, Burton walked out beyond the school grounds. Scanning the business district, he said, "[It] was practically destroyed by fire and wind and nearly every home was flat. I saw about forty automobiles piled up in one big pile and thought it was probably a garage that had been struck." Scanning the distance in the other direction, Burton recalled, "Every tree left standing and every fence had garments, bedclothes, and household goods blown against the west side of them. It looked like the storm began in the west and traveled eastward. I saw furniture, automobile tops and clothing scattered everywhere and saw people fleeing from town slightly clad." Women covered their bare chests with their hands and strips of cloth, as their dresses had been stripped away. Men abandoned their jackets, shirts and pant legs that had been pinned under debris. Infants and toddlers stood naked, searching aimlessly for their mothers and fathers.

Superintendent C.C. Chapman of the Missouri Pacific Railroad, with Trainmaster Ridion and other officers, sped into De Soto on train no. 4 a few hours after the storm, intent on doing everything in their power to help.[52] They had already picked up and delivered doctors to Annapolis, Missouri, earlier that afternoon. Now, the railroad men had do it all again, helping women and children carry blankets and pillows to the basements of several buildings that the storm had hollowed out.

Survivors slept surrounded by the four underground walls of home basements and gazed up at the evening and nighttime sky, wondering what, if anything, there would be left to do tomorrow. Business owners and other men kept guard over the remains of their merchandise in the business district. Most of the stores and homes appeared as though they had no side walls; the merchandise and furniture had been piled into a heap on the floor with lumber thrown carelessly over it.

Men scoured the town and helped people however they could, fighting fires and trying—often in vain—to find their loved ones. A woman and her small twins were found side by side, dead, in a field outside town. There was little good news from the day, but a woman reported only as Mrs. Bennett had held onto her baby as they were blown into a tree. They remained there until the storm passed. Neither was injured, but two of her other children, Tina May and Marie, aged thirteen and nine, respectively, were among the dead at the De Soto School.[53]

Throughout the afternoon and into the evening, people found dozens of bodies. In total, sixty-nine were killed, thirty-eight of them children in the De Soto School.

6

WEST FRANKFORT, ILLINOIS

THE CALDWELL MINE

West Frankfort, Illinois's, residents were no strangers to hard work and back-breaking labor. Since the early pioneer days of the early 1800s, men there hunted and fished and built small but sturdy houses from timber they felled themselves, and the women dutifully maintained their homes in a struggle against nature itself. West Frankfort and its neighbor Frankfort slowly merged into each other after a railroad line intersected with connections to Chicago and Memphis in 1894. Nothing changed life in West Frankfort like the railroad did. With its arrival, pioneer life gave way to coal—and lots of it—by 1917.

The Deering Coal Company brought 3,500 new men and their families to the area after new coal tipples and mines opened in 1917. West Frankfort had the largest coal mine in Illinois, and the Orient no. 2 mine, three miles northwest of town, was the world's largest at that time, churning out 9,500 tons of coal daily.[54]

Thousands of men brought their muscular backs and way of life from across the Midwest and South to search for reliable work shortly after the Civil War, no matter how dangerous and suffocating it could be. Like lead miners in Annapolis, Leadanna and points to the west, coal miners went underground to chisel and haul out the nation's fuel. Conveyor belts carried coal up as much as one hundred feet, and large tipples reached into the sky as much as fifty feet when adjusted for the tallest railroad cars. For men working underground, the coal tipples represented massive feats of human achievement, visible for miles in all directions in the relatively flat basin leading to the Mississippi River.

Despite the dangers, Black men began to apply for work in the mines, too. This new generation of Black families could still recall the horrors of slavery, which had ended just six decades earlier. A new generation of the Ku Klux Klan thrived in Franklin County, too. In 1867, local resident Aaron Neal, among the first members of the national Klan, established the organization in the county. All the ingredients for the Klan were still there, with an inflow of southern and poor white people, a steady movement of Black people and an unstable, close working environment.

Still, Black men pursued mining to support their families, often at greater risk in an already dangerous job. Black miners were among the first in and last out, working in the most dangerous parts of the mines farthest from the entry and exit points and for longer hours and less pay than their white counterparts. They also lived in the bleakest housing.

Workers in the northern end of West Frankfort, near the mammoth New Orient Mine, called the area "new town." It was a large subdivision of about five hundred small, humble houses made of wood with small foundations. The Caldwell mine had one hundred or so men with nearby housing that more closely resembled a camp, with small huts and wooden shacks and dwellings framed around Mine no. 15, three miles northeast of town.

W.A. Brewster, a supply clerk for the mine, was writing at his desk in the supply house when "the wind and hail came, then the bricks began falling out of the walls." It was 3:00 p.m. "The door blew in and I was lifted over the wooden grating along the aisle and fell in the aisle with the grating on top [of] me. That grating saved me from being killed, because the bricks fell in over it. My foot was sticking out, and it got mashed. Otherwise, I was only bruised and scratched. There were three or four others working here, and they were blown outside."

A.E. Crowder, known to his men as the "top boss," since his responsibilities included operations on the surface, was aboveground near Mine no. 15 when the tornado blew in with thunderous devastation.[55] He recalled to a reporter, "It [blew] me out the door of the supply house, plumb across that big refuse dump and the road." He landed on the edge of a pond 150 yards from where he was originally standing. Crowder was pulled from the edge of the pond with several broken ribs. He was found alongside five corpses.

Over five hundred feet below ground, Robert McPhall, or the "bottom boss" of the mine, heard a sudden commotion. He and dozens of other men near the entry shafts stopped working, hushing each other to hear a better sense of what was happening aboveground. "It felt like the wind was blowing right through the bottom," said McPhall. "The electric lights went off, and we had to rely on our carbide lamps."

McPhall called up above on the wired phone that connected the workers to the surface to ask what was happening. He was told calmly by clerk Brewster that a storm was coming.

Then the calm broke. The wind blew the airshaft door open and reversed the draft in the mine, sucking air, dust and soot out of the shafts. Men hurried around the fans, which were quickly shut off to settle the dust. Oxygen deprivation became an immediate danger as nervous men looked around and squinted in the dark. The darkening skies above made the already dim mines as black as the coal in them.

News of the mysterious disaster traveled ahead to the end of the mine works about a mile and a half from the shaft openings. Most thought there must have been an explosion. The power of the storm's concentrated pressure drops and gusts blew the cribbing off the supporting I beams, causing some of the buntons to fall. Fearing the whole mine might collapse if more support beams fell, mine manager Louis Waldron ordered everyone out. Gossip traveled up and down the shafts quickly as all five hundred hundred men traversed the dark pathways with dim carbide lamps and their sense of touch. Noxious gas and carbon dioxide from the earth, equipment and exhalations began to build, causing some men to become dizzy and faint.

At 3:00 p.m. aboveground, forty men were working in the engine room, manning the system devised to keep the rocks and coal conveyors running. Charles Sinks, a weighman for the union, and John Knight, a weighman for the company, were directly on top of the steel tipple, eighty feet up, when the wind started to howl. The storm's outermost winds toppled the entire apparatus in a matter of seconds, seriously injuring Knight, who suffered three broken ribs, one of which likely punctured a lung, and a broken collarbone. Sinks was killed by the crushing debris.

More than two dozen train cars that were sitting on the tracks just under the tipples shook and rumbled under the weight of hundreds of tons of coal awaiting shipment. Moving at about sixty-three miles per hour, the tornado's iron wind scooped up every lump of coal from the train cars and scattered it into the countryside like heavy, black hail. Train engines weighing as much as eighty tons jostled and moved up and off the tracks like great rolling boulders.[56]

Jim McGowan was in the engine room alongside three dozen or so other men when the building's ceiling and brick walls caved in. It took all day and night for men to dig McGowan out brick by brick. Miraculously, only four men inside the engine room were killed. A dump cart driver, Charles Deaton, was crushed when the tipple fell over. Bill Norris, a blacksmith helper, was also caught under the main shaft in his machine shop when he went to retrieve some wheels for carts. Most of the men escaped with only cuts and bruises.

Members of their families were not as lucky. As every man belowground crawled out over the span of forty minutes, they discovered their humble town had vanished. Nine bodies were found huddled around a coal stove in a nearby restaurant.[57] Three generations of the Karnes family hunkered together on the edge of the Caldwell Mine as the storm blew over. Isaac "Ike" Karnes lost his wife, a daughter, a son-in-law, a daughter-in-law and seven grandchildren, their ages ranging from a few months to seven. Isaac Karnes lost eleven family members in two or three minutes.

Ike Karnes's wife and three of the children were picked up along with their home's roof and blown some 2,300 feet away into a pond next to the dam, where Crowder was also found. Ike's sons Roscoe and Tim were the family's sole survivors, as they were in the mine during the storm. They searched in vain for the place they called home and found only piles of broken wood.

Carpenter Perry Dees was working in the mine yard when he saw the thick, boiling cloud come down from the hill. "I called to Boyd Hunter," he recalled. The two rushed to safety, but "the wind threw me under a truck." Another large truck tumbled over, striking Dees's head. Dees fell to his side and clung to the ground; Boyd landed nearby. The two prayed, "Oh, Lord—oh, Lord, save us. We're all gone!" Fearing for his life as the tornado shredded everything and everyone around them, Dees prayed for his wife and two children.

Hunkering under trucks, the two heard the groans of the generating room straining and collapsing under the weight of the wind and debris. First Engineer James Smith came through the wreckage largely unscathed and yelled, "Lend a hand, boys!"

Springing up against the strong winds and dust blowing out from the debris and mines, they found Zeke Taylor crumpled amid the collapsing building. Taylor's body was covered up to his shoulders in a quicksand of steel, wood, brick and dust.

Unable to help, Dees ran home to find his wife and five children still in a standing structure that resembled their home, despite its windows being blown out and much of its exterior loosened or blown away. Dees's other son Rupert and his family lived nearby. When Dees ran to check on them, he found his son's house, wife and baby had been blown away.

In the search for his daughter-in-law and grandson, Dees found Joe Hand's wife and their eighteen-month-old baby dead. After reaching for a nearby blanket amid the rubble, he wrapped his wife and baby together and laid them to rest. As Dees continued to search, his son Rupert and his family walked up. They, along with Dees's mother-in-law, Mary McGowan, had almost all their clothes and shoes ripped off by the force of the wind. His father-in-law, Jim McGowan, was found dead.

Oiler Stanley Reed was walking behind a dump cart driven by another man. "Help me upload this powder to keep it from getting wet," Reed said, jumping on the cart to protect the explosives.[58] The rain picked up and suddenly poured in torrential, horizontal sheets.

Spooked by the storm and figuring his life was worth more than a cart of powder, Stanley hollered, "Hell, there's plenty more!" He fled into the sand house when it was immediately shredded and blown away. The wind, roaring with relentless strength and power all around him, pushed and rolled Stanley along the ground. The cart driver was killed. Unprotected and grasping for protection, Stanley felt there was nothing strong or secure enough to grab onto. The wind then picked up a mule twenty five feet away and dropped it on top of Stanley. The weight of the mule broke his shoulder and slightly fractured his skull. Another man named Denton was working nearby when the storm arrived, and he was also hit by the mule, which crushed his head and immediately killed him.

After the storm subsided, Reed rushed home to find his car sitting out front. "Nothing was left of my automobile but the radiator." Darting inside, he found what was left of his home after the kitchen was shaved off its side. Reed discovered his family and children huddled together in the bedroom.

Stanley Reed's seventy-year-old grandmother, Nola Reed, was gathering kindling for the supper fire when "a black cloud sort of gathered," she recalled. After she shuffled into the bedroom, the windows were immediately blown away. Moving toward the kitchen, she couldn't get the door to budge. The wind held it shut so tightly that she could only listen as her kitchen was dismantled.

Sitting by the kitchen door, the elderly Reed began to pray. "Oh, Lord, take me if you want, but my sons Herman and Clabe are down in that mine. Spare my boys. Give them another chance." When it was over, Mrs. Reed found her kitchen a mass of plaster, timber and stuff blown in from all over the countryside. She survived and so did her sons.

Everyone that Wednesday afternoon prayed, often with more ferocity than they ever thought possible. Mrs. I.L. Perkins, the wife of the minister of the only church near West Frankfort, was visiting a parishioner, Mrs. Dave Price, and her daughter Agnes Price when the storm hit. Feeling the growl of the storm swelling around them, they ran to another house. "Agnes!" said Mrs. Perkins as she began to cry. "Oh, Lord, I ain't saved. I've been a sinner!" cried Mrs. Price. The women huddled together and prayed. Amid the tornado's havoc, Mrs. Perkins told her about salvation, and all three were spared.

Curtis Stagner was in his cottage with his mother when the roof over the bedroom was lifted away, tearing apart everything inside but leaving the bed perfectly unharmed. Stagner watched from the remaining half of his house as a calf was lifted and carried over a wire fence as if by heavenly mana and resettled fifteen yards away.

Next door, a house with five children and their mother was demolished, but no one was hurt. Only the sewing machine and a small section of the floor remained. A rooster was found alive, hurled against a tree near the Caldwell Mine no. 18; its beak had been driven so deeply into the bark that it couldn't escape.[59] Bulls had their horns cleaved from their skulls. Stories of these freakish instances cropped up everywhere across the countryside. Survivors stumbled in shock through the scarred streets and dirt paths for hours after the storm. They appeared weary and subdued but not vanquished.

Between half and two-thirds of the homes in "new town" had been blown to splinters or brushed cleanly away by the storm. The tornado's fight over this place had ripped nearly everything from the earth. The valuable superstructure of the New Orient Mine, owned by the Chicago, Wilmington and Franklin Coal Company of Chicago, was not completely wrecked. But estimates placed the damage to the property at $100,000 or more. The tipple, screener and all other surface property at Mine no. 15, owned by the Industrial Coal Company of Chicago, were completely blown over, bent and distorted beyond repair.

Mrs. Ben LeMasters was driving a taxi between West Frankfort and Orient when the storm struck her car just west of town.[60] The mighty wind sent the car tumbling over itself, ejecting her from the driver's seat and dragging her along the road for hundreds of feet. A large stick was hurled against her and driven straight through her arm. At the Elks Home field hospital, a physician removed the stick. He had to plunge his entire hand through the wound to remove the splinters and dirt.

Among the patients who arrived at the newly improved hospital in the Masonic Hall was Ralph R. Johnson, a Chicago and Eastern Illinois Railroad fireman who had suffered serious hip injuries in the storm. He was home when he saw the wind scoop up eight houses "like a man playing shinny cracks a tin can." Johnson was hurled against a kitchen cabinet. "I grabbed my little girl, Nellie [three], under one arm and Ralph [ten months] under the other, and Juanita [five] caught around my neck with her arms. We went up in the air at least 100 feet and across the electric wires." They landed in a ditch 350 feet away and rolled down 20 more feet before they were stopped against a wall of wind and mud. "All the kids were around me, only scratched but so covered with dirt they looked like pigs."

"There were hunks of fire as big as your head flying through the air," recalled Johnson. "My wife and oldest child were blown out of the house but not hurt. A man came up to me and said, 'Look at that horse—it was blown a mile.'" Johnson and the man took a pair of shafts still fastened to the horse off of it, and it calmly walked away.

As the storm struck, two boys were fishing near the railroad in a little pond. There were freight cars that had been blown off the tracks all around. The two boys were too scared to stop fishing, but by divine providence, the funnel completely missed them.

Others were not so fortunate. All 250 pounds of John Cooper couldn't shut the back door against the tornado in a boardinghouse near the New Orient Mine. He was rolled out of the house just before it was blown away. A man on the second floor was not hurt, but Cooper was pummeled with debris and severely injured.

At the Moore School near the mine, one of the teachers allowed her children out when the storm approached, thinking it safer for them to be home than at the school. But one of the Karnes boys—the son of Isaac Karnes, who lost nearly his entire family—was in that class and was running home when the wind blew over. The storm encircled the students' young bodies as they were swiftly blown into a pond. Those who stayed at the school all escaped serious injury. Little Bert Dunford moved from his seat in class just in time to escape falling plaster. His sister Vera was at home with their mother. Vera told a reporter for the *St. Louis Post-Dispatch*, "Believe me. I prayed, and I'm not ashamed of that. I thought the world had come to an end."

Otto Bagley, a railroad yardmaster and the brother of West Frankfort's mayor, was working in the yard office when he saw the tornado coming.

Several of the people who were inside were hurled through the air for yards and lived to tell of their experience.

"I saw the tornado coming and warned the three others in the office to get out," Bagley said. "Just as I was leaving the building, the rush of wind picked me up as if I were a feather, twisted me around, and dropped me in a ditch forty feet away, in which there was three feet of water. I was stunned but was conscious enough to keep my head above water. I was bruised by a plank which hit me while I was in the air. Otherwise, I wasn't hurt."[61]

In all, seventy-four train cars were blown off their tracks, some as far as one hundred yards—a crucial measurement Weather Bureau researchers used to determine the tornado's wind speed was about two hundred to three hundred miles per hour.

In a twist of good fortune for Hiram Eshelman, a traveling salesman for an undertaking company, the train he was riding in from Greenfield, Indiana, to West Frankfort was delayed a short distance from town because a freight train in front of it was at a standstill for some unknown reason. The delay was a dreary, monotonous affair, but it likely saved his life. While he waited for the train to move, the tornado destroyed his destination. An experienced undertaker, he immediately got to work after reaching what was left of West Frankfort.[62]

In all of Franklin County, including the nearby ruined hamlet of Parrish, the total number of known dead exceeded 160. "I did not remember anything after the storm struck until I found myself holding a fence post

A tent erected in West Frankfort, Illinois, for relief work. *Jackson County, Illinois Historical Society collections.*

a quarter of a mile from the house," remembered Everett Parks, who lived half a mile outside Parrish. "I saw my little boy in the air, only a few feet above the ground, and coming directly toward me. I reached and was barely able to grasp him by the leg. I pulled him down to me and held him until the storm had passed."[63]

Another four hundred were injured, including three hundred in and around West Frankfort. A hasty survey conducted by workers connected with District Relief Commission and Insurance resulted in an estimated total of $1.7 million worth of property damage in West Frankfort, including damage to the two mines.

The houses at the Caldwell Mine belonged mostly to the company, but many miners in the New Orient district owned their own homes. It was estimated that the average loss to a home-owning family there was about $3,500—a ruinous amount for a family who earned only a few hundred dollars a year. The mining company, realizing the supply beneath the earth was dwindling, mostly decided to cut their losses and move on. West Frankfort would never be the same.

7

POSEY COUNTY, INDIANA

GRIFFIN

Eleven-year-old Mary Aline Runyon hopped in her father's mule-drawn wagon to go to school. Her father, Noah, and Tom Ridens, a family friend, took their place in the front and side spring seat. She sat behind her father on the wagon's seat board, and a team of two mules—Kate and Captain—snorted at the ready. But before taking off that morning, Noah reached down for a blacksnake whip that had been lying on the ground all winter.

"What are you going to do with that?" Ridens asked. Mr. Runyon had developed a reputation around Posey County for never using a whip on any animal. He never allowed any hired man to whip his mules or horses either.

Putting the long black whip up front alongside a few other tools and barely pursing his lips, he stoically replied, "Something tells me I will need it before the day is gone."

The ride into Griffin was gray, deeply cloudy and sultry. Located just over the Wabash River and the Illinois border, the town was populated by 350 people who humbly went about their lives. Mary clung to a few of her books and looked wistfully out at the clouds from the backseat. Rain sprinkled overhead a time or two, but the high humidity caused her thick, blonde hair to stand on end. She was dressed in a raincoat to shield her lovely white dress; beige, knee-high socks; and a matching brown belt and shoes, and her father dropped her off at school on the outskirts of town before heading on with Ridens to purchase some supplies.

All day long, wagons and trucks loaded with feed, grain, bedding and goods of every kind rolled up and down the roads in and around Griffin, throwing up showers of gummy mud the color of rich Corinthian leather. Rain and a few gusts of wind had come and gone in spurts. Inside the Griffin school, word came down from Principal Shaw that the students had better get home. Mr. Shaw had witnessed the barometer outside his office window falling all day. Something stirred within him around 3:30 p.m., and he thought everyone should get a move on.

Mary Aline hurried into town to meet her father by George Doll's general store, like they always did each afternoon. Darkening clouds simmered over the horizon. "Hurry!" her father yelled as he saw her come around the corner. Confused and worried, Mary Aline thought she was already walking faster than she thought possible. "But it wasn't fast enough to suit Dad," she recalled later.

"That dark cloud looks bad," Mary Aline called out to her father as he helped her up into the spring seat of the wagon. 'We'll about drown," she worried as the mules began kicking and snorting.

"That's not what worries me," Mr. Runyon said as torrents of rain began to fall.

After Mr. Runyon signaled the mules to take off to the south, the wagon moved at a fast clip. Passing by the Wilson house, Mrs. Wilson yelled out, "Let Mary stay here! You will drown!"

"I can't stop—we've got to get home!" Mr. Runyon cried back. Mary was scared and transfixed by the intensity of her father yelling at the mules and staring straight ahead; something seemed to overtake him. At a furious speed against the pelting rain, Mary looked back at the dark background of the sky. The pillars and clouds of dirt-choked wind surrounded by gray mist grew larger. The trees swayed like tall grass, and sheets of level rain drove the droplets and small hail into their bodies.

Farther ahead, John Delashmit saw the wagon moving by and yelled again for them to stop, offering the refuge of his home and barn. "I can't, John. We've got to get home," Mr. Runyon replied intensely. The rider spurred his mules hard in a race for cover. Gusts of winds threatened to push them out of the wagon and off the road.

The wind shifted direction from the southwest to the southeast, blowing straw from Mr. Delashmit's toward the wagon, scaring the mules into turning around. Intent on getting home as quickly as possible, Mr. Runyon reached down near his toolbox and picked up the blacksnake whip he had stowed away that morning. Snapping the whip into the air and onto the mules' hindquarters, he urged them straight south until they reached the gravel road that led to their farm.

Perhaps noticing the fear in Mary's eyes and voice, Mr. Runyon turned his head halfway toward his daughter. "There's going to be a terrible storm. I saw one when I was seven years old. I've never forgotten it."

Indeed, Mr. Runyon had woken up that morning with the sense that a storm like the one he experienced in his childhood was on its way. "If not for the [mule] team, we'd lie down in the ditch. But we can't let them be hurt. We've got to get home."

When he wanted to drive faster, Mr. Runyon usually kicked the front of the wagon—but not today. Keen to protect every form of life in his charge, Mr. Runyon cracked the whip and rolled the wagon as fast as Mary Aline could ever remember. The rain and wind whipped around in all directions. "My raincoat was unbuttoned, but I couldn't button it, for it took all my time holding on the seat," she recalled. As the seat bounced and rattled with the wagon's intense speed along the divots and holes in the road, it could take no more; its front hook came off the wagon's edge, leaving it to bounce and shift wildly with each turn and bump. "Just hold on, we can't stop," Mr. Runyon said, his eyes fiercely committed to the road.

"Tell me where the clouds are," Mr. Runyon yelled. Since her father was unable to take his eyes off the road, Mary Aline turned and looked around as the rain pierced her face and eyes from every direction. Everything appeared black, but glancing back, she could recognize the clouds were drawing close. "They're not far back of us!" she cried. A look of fear settled on her face.

Behind them, the tornado's immense black fog appeared like a majestic, towering figure from the Old Testament. As the pair approached a gap in their fence line, they saw Mary Aline's mother, Cora Runyon, waiting for them after she had seen them come down the gravel road as quickly as the mules could run. "Get in!" Mr. Runyon called out to his wife as she jumped into the back of the wagon. As they traveled the short distance ahead to the barn, the raindrops grew as large as silver dollars, stinging and soaking everyone as if they were hailstones.

"Get inside!" Mr. Runyon yelled above the rain and wind to Mary Aline as everyone hopped down off the wagon. Mary Aline's fingers were white from gripping the seat, and the mules still needed to be unhitched from the wagon. It was about 4:00 p.m.

Mr. and Mrs. Runyon hurriedly released the mules into the barn before joining Mary Aline inside the modest wood-frame home. They huddled together, soaking wet and dripping pools of rainwater on the floor, as the rain began to ease up a bit.

Curious to see what, if anything, the storm had wrought, Mr. Runyon walked outside to look around. Stepping outside after spending only a few minutes in the barn, he paused. "That's the Armstrong place burning," he said, looking and pointing due north as his wife and child stood at the front door. The sense of unease that had guided Mr. Runyon and his family to safety so far this day pushed him to investigate further. In the distance, a large oak tree had blown over. "Things don't look right. I'm going on to the north road to climb up on the blown-down oak to see if I can see anything," he said, glancing back at his family.

Grabbing her toy spy glasses, Mary Aline, along with her mother, headed southwest of the house to a large knoll. Usually, they could see the large grain elevators and the top of the Frazer farm from the knoll. "I don't see anything," Mary Aline said to her mom. Walking back to the house, Mr. Runyon remarked, "I don't see anything."

As they walked back to the barn, they could see that Kate and Captain, the two mules, still felt uneasy about being attached to the buggy. Saddling Kate, Mr. Runyon told his wife and daughter, "If I'm not back by five, hitch Captain to the buggy and come out."

Around 4:45 p.m., the two worried Runyon women went out to the barn to start hitching Captain to the buggy, but the mule refused. "He's smarter than I am," Mrs. Runyon said after the third try to coax him near the wagon. "He senses something I don't, so we'll quit."

Just as the women were about to head back inside, Mary Aline's father rode up on Kate, relieved to have made it back before they left. "Captain would have run off and killed you if you had even got out there," he said, slightly out of breath from riding hard back to the farm. For as far as Mr. Runyon could see, large oaks and spruce trees had fallen and blocked many of the roads and trails. Telephone and electrical wires were down, and thick palls of smoke billowed from distant homes and farms nearer to Griffin.

Unsure of what else to do, Mrs. Runyon prepared supper as the wind shifted from the northwest. It was strong enough to blow out their small lantern around the table. This happened enough times that Mr. Runyon gave up on trying to keep it lit. After a hasty meal, Mr. Runyon gathered the family up to venture out again in the remaining daylight. They walked as far as the railroad, stood there a while and then came home. "I've often wondered why Dad went, as we couldn't do anything," Mary Aline recalled

The remains of the Griffin School in Griffin, Indiana. *Evansville-Vanderburgh Public Library.*

later. "But he'd seen such devastation, I guess he felt like he couldn't bear to sit home, safe and dry and warm."

As daylight turned to night, the air grew cooler. The atmosphere was dark and foreboding, with howling winds that kept Mary Aline awake all night. "I was afraid another storm was coming up," Mary Aline later recalled. "I think I never saw a darker night." Amid the eerily gorgeous sparks and milky dusk, the only light shimmered from the burning fires and embers at the stores and restaurants in the middle of town. While so many others had tried and failed to outrun and escape the tornado, including Sam Flowers in Ellington and hundreds in central Illinois, the Runyons were some of the few who were successful.[64]

In town, March 18, 1925, was the last day of Roy "Chick" Oller's life. A lifelong resident of Griffin, the thirty-six-year-old bus driver served as a corporal in the U.S. Army during World War I. After returning home, he maintained a home for himself; his seventy-four-year-old mother, Elizabeth; and his brother, Ed.

The hot, glassy atmosphere that had settled over the Ohio River Valley began to clear by 4:00 p.m., when Oller started his afternoon school bus route. The bus looked more like a hack wagon with a wood frame body set on top of a truck chassis. The chassis was made of stiff steel, and every hole, divot and bump in the road rattled immediately from the modest rubber tires to the bones and teeth of passengers.

Oller, seated up front under a small awning, felt the rain starting to pick up. The hack wagon had no doors or windows. Students Mary Ashworth, a friend of the Runyon family; Ted McIntire, ten; and nearly a full load of thirty others sat in the back on open-air benches that lined either side of the wagon's wood frame.

After rounding a corner in front of the VanWay home, Oller stopped to let Helen VanWay and two other students off. One of the students, a young boy named Harry, decided to run back and stand on the small ledge that was used to exit the back of the bus, presumably to talk to friends or stand under the meager metal roof until the rain passed.

It seemed the clouds were moving fast enough that whatever shower this was would blow over in a few minutes. The rain darkened with a dense intensity that reduced Oller's line of sight to mere feet in front of the bus. Deciding the rain might get worse before it got better, Oller made the decision to wait a bit before carrying forward.

Charging ahead, the skies blackened into an inky morass. With sudden ferocity, the wind punched across the bus like a brick wall mounted to a freight train, tumbling the bus over until it came to rest on its side. Children in the back were flung out of the open-air windows in all directions. After the bus came to a rest at the bottom of a small crest, the agonized screams and cries of pain from kids trapped under steel bars and wreckage pierced the air. Ethel Carl and Helen Harris, both about twelve years old, were pinned under a tire. Bus driver Oller was pinned under the front right tire. As the bus rolled, he was expelled onto the ground, and the bus came to a standstill on his hips and abdomen.

The storm's ceaseless funnel charged down the same street as the school bus at an astonishingly rapid seventy-three miles per hour. Nearby buildings were hit like they had been knocked by a mile-wide hammer. Mary Lou Kokomoor was sitting at a table with her brother George and their mother as they prepared for the dinner service at their restaurant. The mean gale suddenly and violently stripped away much of the building's roof and walls, sending a flood of patrons and staff careening into the basement before they were buried alive by falling debris and bricks. The hot stoves and ovens spilled their glowing contents into the morass of twisted bodies and tinder, igniting a blaze that began to spread, despite the falling rain dripping into the crevices.

Lucille Stallings was in George Doll's general store and turned just in time to see a barrage of rain, wind and hail pelting the doors and windows. Hearing the building's wood frame creak and groan under the storm's surging winds, Doll grabbed Stallings and made her way to the back, where she ducked behind the large safe that sat like an immovable iron wall. The two huddled together and placed their faith in the strength of the four-foot-tall safe as blades of rain and shrapnel whipped against the unprotected side of their bodies until the building collapsed onto their unprotected heads.

Blacksmith George Westheiderman was in his shop when the tools hanging overhead and on the walls began vibrating. A large tree collapsed into his shop, unable to withstand the three-hundred-mile-per-hour winds. With steel, iron and molten ore, the funnel inflicted cruel punishment as it blew Westheiderman against a tree and cleaved rods, pipes, tongs, hammers and tools from his shop walls, turning them into shrapnel and projectiles. A foot-long steel pipe shot through the air and pierced Westheiderman just between the ulna and radius bones of his left arm, pinning him to the tree.

Within a few minutes, 210 people—about 60 percent of the 350 residents of Griffin—lay dead or dying. Up in the hills above the valley, the Runyons could do nothing but look out over the desolation as the clouds cleared almost as fast as they had darkened. A light rain turned into a drizzle as survivors walked around in a mental fog and physical nightmare. Death was all around them now, seeping into the soil. The murmuring moans of the weary and injured turned to the shrieks of panic and last gasps for oxygen as fire closed in on trapped survivors.

Back at the school bus, men with just enough wherewithal to act raced toward the terrified screams of schoolchildren who were trapped under the weight of what was left of the wagon. Since most of the children were frozen in shock and terror, it was hard to discern who was alive and who was dead. The wood frame of the bus had been cleanly lifted away, leaving twisted metal and bodies. Only the steering wheel and driver's seat remained recognizable.

While Chick Oller tried to wrestle free from the tire and steel rim, men rushed to his side. "Get the kids! Get the kids!" he insisted, as the volunteers turned their attention to lifting children out from under the wreckage. Children who had been flung out of the bus were thrown in all directions for yards, with deep lacerations gushing blood over their faces and arms. Student Dale Hyatt suffered a broken arm. Broken legs were visible to those first on the scene. With few supplies available, people began hoisting children into blankets, sheets and onto any flat surface they could find lying

Top: An unknown residential area in Griffin, Indiana. *Willard Library collections.*

Bottom: Survivors gather amid their homes in Griffin, Indiana. *Willard Library collections.*

around. Three children lay dead from their wounds. The inconceivable wind speed had stripped all the children of their shirts, dresses and pants. Yet the wind had covered them so thoroughly with mud and debris that they were indistinguishable. Bus driver Oller, terrified for the children and powerless to help, reportedly told the men who were trying to free him, "Let me be, and care for the children."

Four children rescued from the school bus, Ethel Carl, Ruby Cleveland, Helen Harris and Helen VanWay, who was just outside her home when the storm hit, died the next day from injuries they sustained in the rollover and crushing weight of the bus. Just a short distance west of the VanWay house, where the bus had parked, a ramshackle crib stood seemingly unbothered by the storm. It's likely if Oller had continued west for a bit, he and the children could have survived.

Parents searched for their children into the darkening evening hours. Doom itself gripped the hearts of mothers and fathers for hours, sometimes days, relaxing at length only to reveal death, ruin and more heartache when a dead child was found. Many more overlooked their children, unable to discern any recognizable characteristics among the living or dead. Ted McIntire's father was among the first parents to get to the grisly scene. Ted was conscious, but a deep laceration on his head had turned crusty and dark. A child blinded by the dust and mud came along with them, wearing only black sateen bloomers after her skirt was torn away. "Dad, she's wearing a ring. Look!" Ted proclaimed to his father, who, until then, thought the random child was a boy. It was young Ted who correctly identified the young girl as his sister. She remained frightened in silence and terrified at the dark and blurry world before her. It would be months before her vision recovered.

Nearby at the general store, George Doll and Lucille Stallings survived behind the safe. Winfred Fisher, twenty-one and the only boy in his family, was inside with his uncle William Fisher; father, John Fisher; and mother.

Doll awoke with searing pain and blindness, unable to see much of his store, now crumpled around him and strewn for miles. His eyes had been pelted with so much fine debris and grit that his vision was plunged into a muddy darkness. Doll's wife, Blanch, emerged from under the wind-swept debris of her home down the street to see Mr. Stinson walking amid the ruins of the town. "Oh, Mr. Stinson, go tell George our home is blown away!" she cried in such shock and terror that she failed to notice everything else in town was also gone.

Calmly explaining the situation to her, Mr. Stinson said it was like she had awakened from a dream. Running to the ruins of the store as quickly as she could, Blanch could hear the cries for help from her husband and Ms. Stallings. Mrs. Doll picked, hacked and dug at the rubble until her fingers bled, eventually freeing the two. George's vision recovered slowly over several months.

Winfred Fisher died in his mother's arms just after the tornado struck. He was crushed by collapsing debris as he tried to rescue his uncle William

Top: The Schultz Home on Griffin's Main Street rolled on its side. *University of Southern Indiana–Rice Library collections.*

Bottom: Survivors and volunteers walk through the remains of Griffin, Indiana. *Willard Library collections.*

Opposite: Residents and volunteers work to remove debris from Main Street in Griffin, Indiana. *Evansville-Vanderburgh Public Library.*

from under the wreckage. Meanwhile, his father lay nearby, seriously injured in the collapsed store. His mother, in pain, held her son while he bled out from his injuries. The Fishers' only remaining child, America Fisher, a home economics teacher in Cynthiana, was out of the storm's path.

In the basement of a nearby house, a family piano fell through the floor and into the basement, where it landed on top of a young girl. Next door, Blacksmith George Westheiderman, a big, strong ox of a man, stood pinned against a tree with a pipe in his arm. He worried so feverishly about his wife and kids, he wrestled the pipe out of his arm with sheer fortitude, despite the agonizing pain. Hobbling next door toward the young woman under the piano, he attempted to lift the instrument, but the pipe injury to his arm rendered him incapable of supporting the frame's intense weight. It was not until another man by the name of Young came by that the piano was hoisted away, but by then, it was too late. She was dead.

A thick column of smoke towered into the air from the restaurant. It was visible for miles around Griffin. Men hurriedly poured water on the blaze with whatever they could find. The toppled stoves and coal ignited in the basement. Each moment, the conflagration grew, threatening to incinerate trapped survivors. Young George Kokomoor yelled out to his mother

Above: The remains of a filling station in Griffin, Indiana. *University of Southern Indiana–Rice Library collections.*

Opposite, top: A residence and damaged tree in Griffin, Indiana. *Willard Library collections.*

Opposite, bottom: An unknown location in Griffin, Indiana. *Willard Library collections.*

from under the restaurant's collapsed frame. He thought he saw daylight from under several feet of debris. "Try and get out," she instructed with a maternal calm as bricks and debris stood between him and fresh air. Perhaps if he could get out, he could help free his mother and sister.

The restaurant's basement increasingly became an oven threatening to incinerate everyone inside. Everyone who rushed to their aid was fueled by adrenaline. All anyone had left was instinct when local man Slim Combs pleaded with the brigade of men hauling buckets of water to stop. "Stop! Stop!" he cried, realizing the steam generated off the hot coals and lumber was making everyone under the debris worse off.

George Kokomoor managed to claw through to the top of the rubble and was at once lifted to safety by Slim and other men who were working to control the blaze. His mother and sister Mary Lou remained trapped in the incinerating debris. Every bit of combustible rubble ignited, inhaling all available oxygen and leaving none for the survivors. If the oxygen depletion

did not end the lives of everyone, including Virgil Horton and Lester Price, who were also assumed to be inside the restaurant, the fire did. No sign of Virgil Horton was ever found.

Peering around, residents found there was almost nowhere to turn. The devastation was so thorough that Griffin joined Biehle and Annapolis as one of the three towns in the storm's path deemed "100 percent destroyed." Within six days, things would somehow get worse.[65]

8

GIBSON COUNTY, INDIANA

OWENSVILLE AND PRINCETON

The tornado left Griffin for Owensville, Indiana, at its peak speed of seventy-three miles per hour. A few stores, farm supply operations and restaurants and dozens of humble farm homes seemingly evaporated as the storm passed. Farmers discovered trees with up to fifty feet of roots ripped straight up and out of the ground like toothpicks on a serving plate. Homes, telephone wires, churches and landmarks vanished so quickly that survivors who walked the streets afterward became disoriented, unsure of where they were standing in relation to what was once their homes.

Dozens of rooftops and sides of buildings, pieces of sheet metal and glass windows spun off into the air, fluttering from a distance like confetti or glimmering pieces of paper that appeared almost magical.

Fred Trenk returned to his home in Indianapolis's northside Meridian-Kessler neighborhood late on March 18. He told his wife how he had seen multiple funnels hours earlier that afternoon on his way through Gibson County. As Trenk described it, he was driving toward Princeton, Indiana, late in the afternoon when he saw three men walking along a dusty stretch of highway. The three men jumped in his car when Trenk offered them a ride.[66]

The four men drove south for miles as the sky darkened, rain began pelting their windshield and wind shook the auto's metal frame. At about two miles wide and traveling between sixty-five and seventy-five miles per hour, the tornado had the jump on Trenk and his passengers. The debris being flung out and around the center of the storm at nearly two hundred miles or more per hour included metal sheeting, mud, glass, steel, building materials, timber and thousands of pieces of people's livelihoods and memories.

"We gotta get out of here," one man remarked. Trenk slammed on the brakes. All four men rushed out of the car and onto the ground near an embankment. Describing the scene to a reporter later, Trenk said, "It was just a puff and a whir, and then it was over. But we learned later that the tornado's force had been great enough to shatter a four-story factory building and throw fragments of it all over the city."

Trenk's automobile was blown against an embankment along the side of the road a few hundred yards from where they left it. After the storm passed, the men found debris and rocks strewn about, telephone poles down and barns blown down.

"It came out of a clear sky," he declared. "I looked up and saw the whirling cloud, and that was the first warning. We all leapt from the car then and were no sooner on the ground, lying in the mud, than it struck." Giving up on their trip, Trenk and the three other men turned the car around. Hours later and about seventy-five miles away, the men noticed all along the way between Crothersville and Seymour, along U.S. 50, telephone poles, barns and trees blown over, uprooted and splintered. This damage in rural Washington and Jackson Counties was not the work of the same tornado but was the result of the same mesocyclone that had spawned its last gasp of a tornado.

Willard Williams was in his barn five miles southwest of Owensville, Indiana, a little before 4:00 p.m. In his house, seventeen people were milling around in preparation for dinner in the home's basement, six of them children just home from school. James Waters, a family friend, was visiting upstairs when he looked out to witness the gently rolling hills of southern Indiana bathed in darkness.

An immense wedge of sheer terror punctuated by flashes of lightning appeared over the horizon. Its power unchallenged, it rotated in a thick, black fog that appeared solid as an anvil. Yet it proceeded almost quietly. Minutes before striking, almost like a wolf stalking its prey, the storm pounced from near silence into a ferocious attack. Ceaseless and unrelenting, the force of the winds charged on, as if a freight train from hell was parting the skies, affixing people's gaze as they stood frozen in time, awed and unable to move.

Unable to make out a distinct funnel, Waters watched the wind that was swirling all around him until he realized the dust and inky fog outside was filled with debris. Waters was blown out of the house into a nearby ditch, where he could just make out the destruction of a barn, a log house, a few outbuildings and lean-tos and the new farm home built by William's father, Dr. J.M. Williams.[67]

Mr. Williams was killed instantly as his barn was lifted off the ground around him. Debris struck him from all sides. Once the wind subsided enough to allow Waters to stand up and collect his thoughts, he ran over to find almost nothing remained of his home except the basement. Among the sixteen people left inside his home, only Franklin Overton, another visitor, suffered an injury. He had a broken hip, as some remnants of the house and debris had been deposited on top of him. Everyone else looked up to see Waters standing over them from the edge of the foundation.

Back at Waters's own farm, three generations of his family, including his seventy-year-old father, Richard Waters; thirty-five-year-old son, Lemuel; and six-year-old grandson, Budie, died in their home. Brothers William and Walter King and their wives, Elizabeth and Laura, were found dead outside of their home after the storm lifted it from its foundation and scattered it across the countryside. An unidentified infant was also found nearby; no one knew where they came from.[68]

John Davis, a neighbor, remarked, "Last Wednesday, as I stood here, I could see fifteen houses as I looked toward the west. Today, I can see just one."[69]

In tiny Owensville, quick-thinking drivers angled their buses and vehicles into the face of the wind to avoid being rolled over. Francis Wilson and Jeff Higginbottom could see the funnel from a distance and quickly drove the noses of their vehicles into an embankment to save themselves and their passengers.

Eighty-five farms were destroyed around Owensville before the storm passed into Princeton at 4:18 p.m. The once-proud and humble area was now a flat, black stain, its only recognizable feature a gridwork of scarred roads passing nothing and leading nowhere.

Commercial painter Jim Elliott of Princeton was at home with his wife, mother-in-law and four daughters when the tornado appeared overhead. He huddled with his family against the inside front wall of the house. They all shut their eyes and prayed as the storm's force slammed down with intense precision. Looking out over their belongings, they could see the tornado had swept away their doors and windows, much of their furniture, the rug from the living room floor and even the clothes that were hanging neatly in their closet. Their home, however, withstood the brunt of the winds and remained standing, even as the storm stripped bark from the trees in the front yard.[70]

Unlike inhabitants in points farther west, most people in Princeton had already left work or school for the day and were scattered out of the tornado's path across Princeton's south side. The Southern Railway shop was leveled, killing a fireman and a janitor who worked there at night.

The Heinz plant lost most of its third floor, killing 1 worker. The nearby Baldwin Heights School was destroyed, but everyone had long since gone home. In all, 45 people died and 152 were injured in Princeton. It's believed Princeton's downtown square was bustling, too, with shoppers in town for regular Wednesday afternoon sales and out of harm's way.

Like Trenk, dozens of witnesses reported seeing, from the tops of hills near Owensville and Princeton, three distinct funnels twirling along in unison for six miles. These satellite tornadoes were separate funnels, which are rare but most commonly rotate around the periphery of a large, strong mother tornado. When satellite tornadoes occur, they usually spawn near multiple funnels, as witnesses reported on March 18. As the mesocyclone veered slightly northeast, it appeared satellite tornadoes were merging back into the mother funnel. This is usually an illusion as the satellite funnels move behind the larger funnel before lifting into the sky.[71]

Indeed, a lot about how a tornado forms and behaves appears to be an illusion to people on the ground. Ninety percent of tornadoes in the U.S. last long enough to be measured in seconds and produce wind gusts that rank them as EF1 tornadoes on the contemporary Enhanced Fujita scale, in which winds range from 65 to 110 miles per hour. But on March 18, 1925, the masses of air tumbled and snarled together in the sky to form a cyclone with a vortex on the ground that was nearly two miles wide. The tri-state tornado of 1925 had a vortex base on the ground that was wider than most tornadoes' tops in the upper atmosphere.

For over three and a half hours, this storm's mix of tumbling cool and warm air, moisture, evaporation, pressure differences and wind speed lined up in a once-in-a-generation tornado that stretched over 219 miles. The tri-state tornado had changed its camouflage from a foggy battleship gray to a patchy muddy brown as it passed over land until 4:30 p.m., when, near the sleepy outpost of Outsville, Indiana, the tornado struck one last house and then lifted away like a great spirit into the sky.[72] The tornado was gone, leaving in its wake a mass of debris, uprooted trees, lumber, glass and demolished autos, strewn among the skeletons and foundations of buildings and bodies.

FIRST RELIEF TRAINS

5:00 P.M., WEDNESDAY, MARCH 18, 1925

News of the storm made its way into telegraph offices at the *Chicago Herald and Examiner* by 5:00 p.m. After they were told of the storm's unimaginable destruction and misery, reporters and editors huddled around news desks, phones and radios to search for information. No one knew just how large or damaged the devastated area was.

By 7:00 p.m., the *Chicago Herald and Examiner*'s staff had heard enough to begin organizing the first relief train full of whatever could be hastily gathered. The paper commissioned radio appeals early in the evening that brought 125 doctors and 75 nurses and assistants to help those affected. The train left at 10:00 p.m. for the stricken area, filled with a team of 200, plus four Pullman cars in which people could sleep and recover, two baggage cars full of medical supplies and a car full of tents sufficient to establish a tented city.[73]

The appeal had been so urgent, most of the physicians carried only a bag of medical supplies. Some did not even have time to bring a fresh change of clothes. Dozens more physicians and nurses gathered at suburban stops outside Chicago to board the special train. The train was placed in charge of Dr. Thomas A. Carter, a nationally known specialist, and was ready for orders by whoever was already first on scene.

Arrangements were made so hastily that no one knew precisely where to go or if they could even get there by train. In conjunction with railroad officials working on equally scarce information, those who wished to help planned to travel to Centralia, Illinois, an Illinois Central terminal, where railroad officials hoped to have more information for those on board about where to go and how to get there. Most believed the ultimate destination was Murphysboro.

Relief trains were being organized around the Midwest, but railroad officials struggled to ascertain the full scope of the damage. Almost every telephone and telegraph wire lay on the ground, as virtually no poles stood for over two hundred miles. Accurate messages from the disaster zone came mostly from those who passed through or who were just north or south of the area shortly before or after the tornado passed, like the hail-damaged passenger train no. 32 that narrowly escaped the storm in Annapolis.

Operators at the Missouri Pacific Railroad and Red Cross in St. Louis began organizing physicians and aid cars after hearing the news the same evening, but heading east into the storm's track was assumed impossible until it was tried. Train engineers would just have to ride the rail lines slowly and watch for debris or warped tracks. What these first responders found reminded many of their efforts in the Great War just a few years earlier.

From all directions, conductors slowed their locomotives to a crawl. Dark conditions made it impossible to see well, but the unmistakable scents of ozone and death clung to the air. The fields were changed into swathes of iron desolation and death dotted with bodies. Debris stretched awkwardly for miles in all directions, almost like snow that fell in one location but not another. Poles and steel were twisted in fantastically awkward shapes. Fearing the rail lines or a bridge might suddenly fall out from under them, most conductors made it only as far as the outskirts of the most heavily damaged areas. Their supplies would have to be carted in by hand, or the walking wounded would have to come to them.

Elsewhere, survivors with vehicles that had not been destroyed uncovered them from the debris or rolled them back onto their wheels to press them back into service. Thousands of vehicle roofs—often nothing more than a solid canvas top—had been shorn cleanly from their frames. These drivable and distinctive vehicles became known as "tornado convertibles."[74] However, thousands more survivors were completely stranded.

Rescuers on relief trains came into towns overrun with panic and despair. In some cases, the residents of these damaged towns who had escaped injury became panic-stricken and attempted to flee from the disaster scene by running in whatever direction they faced until their legs simply could not go on. At Murphysboro, several frightened people grabbed whatever they could carry and threw themselves aboard a passing train, while in other places, many ran into the fields far from town, screaming at the top of their lungs. However, these panic-stricken people were comparatively few, and many returned later to aid in the rescue.[75] But the psychological fear loomed over everyone.

National guard troops in Illinois arrived in several of the larger towns and attempted to handle traffic. At first, traffic consisted of people trying to return to their homes or flee town. But as news of the storm spread, sightseers who could hardly believe the stories went out to see for themselves and clogged the few passable roads and bridges.

News traveled quickly around the region, despite the conditions and difficulty communicating. Thousands of motorists, eager to see if what they heard on the radio or from neighbors was true, converged into whatever was left of the cities and towns. Martial law was declared in each jurisdiction by nightfall, as guardsmen and policemen—many of whom had lost their own property and loved ones that day—stood watch, directing people without supplies or need to be in the area away.

Looting was a concern for most guards. Tales of pillagers rummaging through debris for jewelry and other valuables and walking off with whatever they could carry were overblown but did exist. In West Frankfort, Illinois, a man was caught taking a ring from a dead woman's finger by a guard, and he was hauled before the captain.[76] Doubtless assuming no jury would convict him, the captain shot the man on the spot.

"Darkness still hampers the agents of mercy tonight," wrote a reporter for the *Chattanooga Daily Times* who traveled north to the area. "National guardsmen have thrown cordons of protection about them. Automobile lights, candles and flashlights are substituting for power plants. Pullman cars have arrived to house refugees in one or two sectors, and villages of tents are arising elsewhere." Where electric light plants had not been destroyed, lights were arranged outside so rescue work might continue at night.[77]

In other towns, bonfires, headlights and hand searchlights were used to aid workers as they dug through the rubble. Determined men found tools and equipment that still worked or could be made to work. Hundreds more walked the streets, looking for bodies to take to makeshift morgues. Railroads used any available car to carry the injured to nearby towns, where hospital facilities were available, and upon their return, they carried back more volunteers in a brigade of mercy.

Isaac "Ike" Levy was a Murphysboro attorney who left town that morning to attend a trial in Jonesboro. He drove back into Murphysboro, only to find his beloved hometown smoldering, soggy and collapsed around him. He drove as close to his home as possible, but the area's debris-clogged roads

A destructive view of Murphysboro, Illinois. *Jackson County, Illinois Historical Society collections.*

made navigating impossible. Deciding it would be faster to walk after he could drive no farther, he found his wife and young daughter alive but visibly shaken and terrified. They told him they couldn't see or hear the tornado coming. The leafless trees created nary a whistle until the relentless force was on top of them.

By nightfall, all the hospitals in Carbondale were overflowing with the injured from Murphysboro, and everyone assumed more people were buried, perhaps alive. Many of the Murphysboro and De Soto rescuers had to give up digging through debris as night fell to combat the flames that broke out in the ruins and threatened to incinerate survivors. For many of the smaller towns and villages hit by the storm, pleas for relief were sent out intermittently whenever a wire could be found to carry a message or an automobile could make its way from the devastated regions to other towns that had escaped the fury of the storm.

The same evening, after the storm, thirty-nine-year-old Dr. Herbert T. Wagner of Indianapolis and Drs. Robert L. Browning and Grant Hartzell, both from Washington, pulled into Indianapolis on a train car with Edith Rieder and Isabel Walker, two Red Cross nurses from the Red Cross's Indianapolis teaching center.[78] The doctors, their wives and the two nurses were there as part of a traveling first aid training team. When a Red Cross messenger rushed in with the news that a great tornado had struck 150 miles away, the medical team ushered students away, shut the train doors

Devastation in Murphysboro, Illinois, at an unknown location. *Jackson County, Illinois Historical Society collections.*

and urged the conductor to make for Griffin with everything the train could handle.[79]

The training car was among the first to arrive in Griffin with stretchers, bandages and other medical supplies. "We found [Griffin] totally destroyed," recalled Helen Wagner, Dr. Wagner's wife and a veteran of the Red Cross. Throwing open the doors, the doctors began treating people who were already lined up. Mothers held wounded babies; men carted injured survivors on doors, wood planks, sheets and mattresses. In the chaos of the response, Mrs. Wagner recalled, "We found no organization for locating missing persons [or] reuniting families." Getting a sense of the scene, Mrs. Wagner said, "When I stepped from the car, a young man saw my Red Cross button and approached carrying a box in which was the skull of a man, and he asked what he should do with it."

Looking around, survivors came wandering in from all corners. Dead animals, including goats, chickens, mules, horses and cattle, were lying everywhere. Dogs and cats lay motionless across soggy fields. What wasn't covered with oatmeal-like mush from pulverized building materials was layered with a gritty film of sand, dirt and debris. Recognizing that locals were in shock and unable to grasp the extent of the catastrophe, Mrs. Wagner and the other physicians' wives on board got to work establishing an information bureau. Until a tent could be erected, a makeshift spot

A small tent city is erected in Griffin as relief workers and volunteers gather. *Willard Library collections.*

outside the train became Griffin's new communications hub. People were to bring a description of the missing to the information tent, and anyone who transported a victim to a hospital in Evansville, New Harmony and elsewhere could leave names and descriptions of who was taken where. The mail could be delivered and sorted, and telegrams could be sent and received, at first through messengers who traveled outside the disaster zone, where service was still available, and later to direct telegraph wires hooked to equipment at the tent.

None of the Red Cross workers were new to this work. Mrs. Wagner and the other members of her nursing crew served during the great flood of 1913 and in World War I. The physicians also relied on their field experience from the war. For his part, Dr. Wagner had been suffering from the flu and soldiered into the stricken area, wobbly legs and all. "I'll remain here until we're no longer needed!" he thundered.

After some time treating the walking wounded, the physicians ventured out from their medical car to check on the people in town and in the fields. Working methodically through the streets, they encountered another Red Cross medical car from Evansville, Indiana. Recognizing they were no longer the only help on the scene, the teams combined forces, and Mrs. Wagner began cross-checking their information sheets of the missing, dead and injured. Working with local police and guard troops that were starting

Top: Timber driven through the stump of a tree in Murphysboro, Illinois. *Jackson County, Illinois Historical Society collections*.

Bottom: A view looking east from the west of Murphysboro after the storm. *Jackson County, Illinois Historical Society collections*.

A scarce train arrives in Griffin shortly after the storm but before the floods in Griffin, Indiana. *Willard Library collections.*

to arrive in town, they ordered the dead animals burned to protect the area's inhabitants against disease.

As the stench of burning livestock and other animals settled in the air, workers coordinated efforts under the leadership of Mrs. Walker and soon discovered more bodies under the debris of homes and businesses. One body was discovered in the ruins of the post office, and it was known there were more under there, but digging them out was time-consuming, powered only by the hands and backs of distraught men and boys who were coming to terms with what sort of evil had inflicted such cruel punishment. The tornado had made shrapnel out of seemingly everything, and injuries to rescuers who were doing their best to avoid stepping on nails or touching hot wires or stoves were just as common as the injuries from the tornado itself.

As precious few bits of news about the missing filtered into the women at the information tent, scant details slowly turned into hunches, and hunches turned into truths. Sure her husband was living, one woman calmly walked up and asked the ladies at the information tent where he might be. "We had to tell her that her husband, her brother and her father were dead," recalled Mrs. Wagner.

A young man, Sid Hiatt, had been reported missing early Friday morning. "Later that same day, another man reported missing came over from Evansville," she recalled. "We asked him if he knew where Hiatt was. He

Officers pose near a truck and tent in Griffin, Indiana, after the storm. *University of Southern Indiana–Rice Library collections.*

had been with Hiatt in a barbershop when the storm broke." Retelling the story, the man said Hiatt ran out the barbershop door, jumped into a coupe and drove up close next to a nearby brick wall for protection. "We sent out a detail and dug into the brick wall," which had collapsed, "and found Hiatt dead in the car."

10

TRIAGE

Sixty miles south of Gorham, Illinois, Dr. Bellenden Seymour Hutcheson, the city of Cairo's leading health officer and physician, heard a knock on his door at 11:30 p.m. on March 18. Strikingly handsome, with a close-cut shave and haircut and strong, broad shoulders, he was informed a terrible storm had destroyed miles of southern Illinois. Hutcheson was no ordinary physician. The forty-two-year-old was born in Mount Carmel, Illinois, and after he graduated from Northwestern University Medical School, he sought to join the army as a medical officer in Europe during World War I. But America was not formally involved. In 1915, Dr. Hutcheson renounced his U.S. citizenship and joined the Canadian army as a medical officer.

Dr. Hutcheson, then thirty-four, was first attached to the Canadian Expeditionary Force's Ninety-Seventh Battalion as a captain but transferred to the Seventy-Fifth Mississauga Battalion. He was then shipped to France.[80]

On September 2, 1918, Captain Hutcheson's unit went through the German defenses at the Drocourt-Quéant support line, the backbone of the enemy's resistance, which included a sophisticated network of interlocking trenches, tunnels, concrete shelters, machine gun posts and dense masses of barbed wire. It also included a light rail system that was used for transporting soldiers, ammunition and other supplies. Suffering heavy casualties and injuries, Captain Hutcheson remained on the battlefield, dodging heavy fire and artillery until every man was cared for. Discovering an officer unable to walk and bleeding heavily, he dressed his wounds under the intense *rap-rap-rap* of machine gun and shell fire. With the help of German prisoners and some of his remaining unit, he evacuated everyone to relative safety. For this, he was awarded the Military Cross.[81]

Looking back to another wounded sergeant, Dr. Hutcheson stood up in full view of the enemy and, armed with nothing but intense devotion to duty and the medical cross on his arm, charged forward and dragged the man into a shell hole, where he dressed his wounds. This act of heroism would earn him the Victoria Cross, the highest, most prestigious award in the British Honours System. The king's official citation declared, "Captain Hutcheson performed many similar gallant acts, and, by his coolness and devotion to duty, many lives were saved."

Hutcheson, part of what became known in Canada as the "Magnificent Seven," was one of only two Americans in 1925 to hold the Victoria Cross. William Henry Metcalf of Maine, who joined the Canadian armed forces against his mother's wishes and served alongside Dr. Hutcheson, was the other. After the war, Hutcheson left Canada and resumed his American citizenship. As if waking up from a dream, he returned home to southern Illinois, where he joined the staff of St. Mary's Hospital in Cairo, Illinois.[82]

Hearing news of the tornado, Dr. Hutcheson grabbed his shoes, coat and other necessities and walked out his front door. He slipped into his fieldwork again and began making preparations to meet the influx of injured patients. A small town of a few hundred nestled into Illinois's southernmost tip at the Mississippi and Ohio River Delta, Cairo did not have much to offer. But it had Dr. Hutcheson. Within an hour of hearing about Gorham, Murphysboro and much of southern Illinois, Dr. Hutcheson had awoken enough of the town to begin lining up ambulances and trucks at the Missouri-Pacific Railroad depot. Anything that could reasonably transport a stricken person was pressed into service.

St. Mary's Infirmary ably served the residents of Cairo, but inside and out, nurses and doctors under Dr. Hutcheson's orders were transforming the modest facility into a field hospital reminiscent of those used in his battlefield treatment work seven years earlier with the Canadian army. Every available bed, wheelchair, blanket, bandage, suture and medical vial was organized, shelved and readied. There was not enough.

The Cairo high school gymnasium, elementary school, city hall and other public buildings were ordered open and supplied with whatever food, water and meager medical supplies that could be found. Residents who had been awoken by the news from neighbors and family rushed to bring whatever useful supplies they might have in their homes. Men filled pails of water, women grabbed cans of beans and stacks of clothing and pillows and children grabbed dolls and toys.

Then they waited. Trucks and ambulances lined up for blocks at the railroad depot and shut off their engines to save fuel. Nurses milled around the medical tents and infirmary, checking and double-checking their supplies. A sense of uneasy calm passed over everyone. Within four hours, residents of the town—many of whom had likely never visited Gorham or any of the other towns in the storm's path—had woken up in the middle of the night and transformed their homes to help.

In Gorham, the special relief train was ready to depart as people fought through the remains of their town to the tracks, which were miraculously still operational. A telegraph operator found two babies lying side by side in a field just outside of town. Both were living and seemingly uninjured. He wrapped his shirt around one and his undershirt around another to keep them dry from the rain. At the same time, on the other side of town, Jim Dunn found his baby injured and not breathing just before the relief train was about to leave for Cairo. While he rushed with his baby in his arms to the train, the baby died. He slowly turned and carried the lifeless body back to the ruins of his home.[83]

At 3:30 a.m., just over twelve hours after the tornado entered Illinois, a special medical train dispatched from Gorham pulled into the Cairo M&O Depot. Trucks and ambulances restarted their engines, and men who had

The Missouri-Pacific Depot in Gorham, Illinois. *Sallie Logan Public Library*.

gathered outside to chat and distract themselves from the chilly air resumed their mounted positions behind their vehicles.

Chugging into a controlled stop, the train's exhaust released a final whoosh of air, and the car doors opened. At once, as many as fifty or sixty people began hollering for help. Limp, bloodied bodies of women and children were carried out by men using nothing but their hands, tattered blankets and makeshift stretchers. Others were moaning and screaming in agonizing pain as metal shrapnel, timber and other debris splintered their bodies. People stood and ambled like exhausted refugees.

Doctors and nurses triaged patients by medical need and transferred each to a waiting ambulance, truck or bus. Drivers peeled out of the railyards one after another for an hour, en route to the hospital or a nearby shelter. Sarah Bean, an elderly woman whose house collapsed around her, crushing her husband and killing many of her children, was among the first to arrive in Cairo.

Calmly and efficiently under Dr. Hutcheson's leadership, nurses and doctors examined the terrified and severely injured patients. The sheer amount of dirt embedded within victims' skin, combined with blood and tears, made examining some patients immeasurably challenging. While working down the lines of patients streaming through the door at St. Mary's, Dr. Hutcheson recognized a man who had been his cook in the Canadian army during the war. Elsewhere, children and families were reunited as they passed near each other in the halls. Five-year-old Fern Vassey thought her three-year-old brother, Roy, was dead. The younger Vassey identified her brother in the hospital, even though he was covered in a bandage wrap. Doctors moved him to his sister's bedside.

Nurses toiled for eighteen hours straight during the initial surge, as medical tents overflowed. An influenza outbreak that was already gripping Cairo threatened to transform the lines of patients on the ground, in tents, under blankets and on every available mattress into corpses. To relieve some of the nurses, civilian women took up the job of checking on patients, wetting washcloths and cleaning linens. Among the initial sixty patients who arrived from Gorham, only four were lost thanks to Dr. Hutcheson's mammoth efforts. The elderly Mrs. Bean was among them; she died four days after the storm, on March 22, 1925. Her injuries, blood loss and heartbreak were too much.[84]

Not giving up the fight, residents of Cairo opened their doors to the children of Gorham who had lost their homes and, often, their parents. The children, they declared, would attend school in Cairo until their school was repaired.

Within two hours of the storm's end, Indiana Red Cross Agent Wright had organized a volunteer party for a special train that left Indianapolis over the Illinois Central Railroad at 9:40 p.m., carrying tents, blankets, water, food and other supplies for southern Indiana.

Marcus S. Sontag, the chairman of the Evansville Red Cross chapter, heard of the storm and immediately began sourcing nurses, doctors and emergency workers in his district immediately south of Griffin and Princeton, Indiana.

Forty miles southeast of Princeton and seven miles south of Griffin, a hasty triage hospital was established in the New Harmony High School gym. Among the first relief workers there was Dr. Wagner of Indianapolis and his wife, who arrived earlier on the special Red Cross training car. Dr. Wagner labored incessantly against disease and injuries. Like many of the survivors who were exposed to the cold, wet and dreary scene, Dr. Wagner, who arrived with flu symptoms, developed a worsening fever and chills until he retired to his home five days later. Dr. Robert L. Browning, the national Red Cross field representative from Washington, traveled back with him, in awe of the physician's devotion to duty, despite his own illness.[85]

Meanwhile, Captain Wald S. Hunter of the Indiana National Guard in Mt. Vernon worked with a dozen of his men and a battery of bulldozers around Griffin. For hours, they turned over debris, ready to rescue survivors for transport to the New Harmony Field Hospital or Deaconess Hospital in Evansville, where nurses stood ready. But Captain Hunter grimly reported they found no survivors.

Fifty of Griffin's injured had already been taken to hospitals and private homes to the south in New Harmony, Indiana. Survivors told grim stories of the scene in Griffin from their hospital beds. "Between groans, they told of how the town is in absolute darkness, except for the ghastly flaring of their burning homes," wrote one reporter.[86]

Broken victims of the storm were wheeled or carried one after another before what few doctors had arrived. Each pronounced the fate of the sufferers after cursory glances and turned to the next. Though hope was often held out, an extraordinary number of amputations were necessary for both expedience and safety.

Residents of the village of Lenzburg, Illinois, located about fifty-five miles northwest of Murphysboro, did not appear to have much to give. Among its 502 residents, the community raised about $447. At less than $1 a person, the meager sum represented a mighty financial strain on a town sustained entirely by mining camps. But what the residents lacked in financial power, they made up for in manpower. Within a day of the storm's passing, 120 men and women rode into Murphysboro and points east and west of the storm's path. The second day saw another 100 and the third still another 100. All told, over half the town picked up what they could carry and moved into town in a show of force not seen near here since Ulysses S. Grant led the Union army south for battle in the Civil War.

In Carterville, ten miles south of Bush, residents raised money to cover hospital bills. A volunteer fire brigade arrived to help extinguish fires, armed with a hose that was never used because all the available fire hydrants were already in use. Many volunteers switched to digging graves. Women collected blankets for victims in De Soto, and since they were so close to Bush and the storm's periphery, many opened their doors to family and friends they knew had lost everything.

So many supplies were collected that by the time Campbell Hill, Illinois residents were about to send their next truckload, word came from Murphysboro: "There's no more room." Large quantities of bedding, food, children's clothing, bottles and other supplies had landed in the stricken areas with nowhere else for them to go. A train car of cabbages arrived over the Missouri Pacific Railroad, and not knowing what to do with them after two days, the relief committee in Murphysboro put out the call: "Go get 'em. They are free." Nearly all the cabbages were taken.[87]

Still, the walking wounded kept coming. A day after the storm passed West Frankfort, thirty-six-year-old James Williams, described as a dirty, ragged man with a bandaged head, staggered into the hastily erected tent of the Disaster Relief Commission and told his story to W. Waldo Shaver, the youthful and super energetic director of the relief work there.

"For God's sake," Williams groaned, "Give me a place to sleep. I was on my porch, near the New Orient Mine, watching the storm. First thing I knew, something hit me, and I rolled away, got up, got knocked down, and rolled again. The house blew away, and they found my wife and baby dead. I tried to help rescue others as long as I could." He fell asleep in a tailor shop until it was closed.[88]

By the next morning, the weather had eased, along with the temperatures. The previous day's highs in the sixties were replaced with morning lows in the thirties and the occasional gust of wind. All through the night and into the morning, the exhalations of the living became visible in the chilled air, serving as a reminder to all who remained that they were still breathing. Running on pure adrenaline and fear, people kept moving without sleep among the hundreds of unburied dead and vile remains of their homes and towns.

Volunteers began placing bodies into neat rows and piles wherever they could find room—basements and the living rooms of damaged but serviceable homes were favored—but often, hastily erected tents were the only choice. Women had given away all their remaining bedsheets and blankets to wrap the dead. Men began digging long, rectangular mass graves where bodies could, for now, be placed without ceremony in the hopes that someone could identify them. Most, however, were beyond recognition.[89]

The wild rush of stampeding wind tore off limbs and seared dirt and debris so deep into people's skin, they appeared covered in tattoos. Even among the living, bruising from being hit by timber and metal lent them a deep purple complexion. Perhaps more debilitating was the number of men and women who had been stripped of everything, including the clothes on their backs. Boys and girls wandered the remains of the streets, naked or with clothing so torn they were held on with threads. Reporter Kenneth Andrews chronicled, "One poor girl was plucked from her own home and whirled through the air into the ruins of another house. On the way, every stitch of her clothing except her stockings was blown off." Despite painful bruising, she was not injured.

Looking around where her house once stood in Griffin, an elderly woman noticed a brand-new automobile parked out front. A passerby remarked, "The storm didn't hurt your new car, did it?" "That's not mine," she replied. "I had a sedan. It's gone. This other came from I don't know where, but it's a pretty good trade."[90]

Despite some good humor among survivors, immense and serious work lay ahead. The Red Cross organized a clearinghouse for survivors to come in to register their name and what, if anything, they knew about missing loved ones. Temporary hospitals became flush with nurses and doctors, many of whom trekked in on foot or rail hand cart carrying whatever they could hold.

In rural areas like Annapolis and Cornwall, Missouri, the mules and horses that survived the storm were put to work hauling food, water and medicine across the debris-pocked land. When there were no more mules or horses to go around, there were men and boys. Scores of Black and white men volunteered their backs to start moving provisions farther into towns like Murphysboro and De Soto. For days, they moved supplies, while others worked to clear or repair the rail lines.

Miraculously, survivors were found. A naked nine-month-old was found half buried in the swampy mud near West Frankfort, Illinois. The child had survived there for two nights, and after receiving a little food and water, it was apparently uninjured from its whirlwind adventure. A woman was found screaming for help by men near her home in De Soto. She sobbed uncontrollably until workers uncovered a baby buggy, where the woman's five-day-old son rested, uninjured.

A calling card belonging to the Reverend H.W. Abbott was lying on the bookcase in his study. The day after the storm, he received a telephone call from a man 210 miles away who said he had picked up the card in front of his house. A check for $800 had been lying beside the card and was left untouched.

With his First Baptist Church destroyed, Reverend Abbott started a brief sermon Friday morning with other Murphysboro church leaders, saying, "This is one of the greatest tragedies that has ever visited the nation. We have the sympathy of a nation. If God is with us, we need have no fear. Let us hope that we may meet death as courageously and heroically as those who perished."

Among the other ministers who addressed the meeting were the Reverend Victor Frohne, formerly an evangelical minister in Murphysboro; the Reverend F.A. McFali, the pastor of the African Methodist Episcopal church; the Reverend Schneider, the pastor of the Lutheran church; and the Reverend Hammond, a former minister of the Methodist Episcopal church, South.

In a unified service, all the church leaders gathered in the two remaining Protestant churches in town to "pray for strength rebuilding the community and ask for light to see the glory to come from all the grief."

One service was held in the partially unroofed First Methodist Episcopal Church. Baptists joined in this service after a new $85,000 church of theirs, set to have been dedicated the next Sunday, was destroyed. Area doctor F.C. Hiller of Thebes, Illinois, was in the new Baptist church with his wife and son when the storm struck. A few minutes into the tornado, the building collapsed on them, killing his wife. At the time of the storm, the grief-stricken doctor held to his oath and urged his son to retrieve whatever surgical instruments he could find so he could start administering medical aid while his wife's body lay beneath the ruins of the house of God. Her body was recovered the next day and buried that Sunday.[91]

Doctors and nurses worked without expecting to be paid. Directors of Evansville's St. Mary's Hospital, Deaconess Hospital and Walker Hospital jointly announced, "Hospitals and the medical and nursing profession are now and will always be dedicated to the service of humanity without the thought of cost, either financial or physical."

Henry M. Baker, the national director of the Red Cross disaster relief program and the man in charge of all Red Cross operations in the tornado zone, told reporters on the evening of March 21, "An emergency unit has been established in every stricken area, and all the injured have received medical attention, and all the homeless have been temporarily sheltered." This would have come as news to dozens of families in rural areas who were still sheltering under lean-tos and huddled around open barrels or righted stoves for warmth.

To the best of the Red Cross workers' understanding, the most pressing relief work was out of the way. Infection stations were set up to isolate potentially infected individuals from everyone else. A separate wound dressing station in each region was established so people who were not in a hospital could have their wounds dressed daily. Plans were underway to make a permanent relief headquarters, since most operated out of small tents or train cars or in the open air. The reality of the rebuilding work ahead loomed larger than the storm itself, and medical units, army distribution, missing persons units, food lines and other relief work would be around for much longer.

11

ANTI-TETANUS SERUM

TWENTY-FOUR TO THIRTY-SIX HOURS AFTER THE STORM

The calls and telegrams came sporadically at first, and then they came in waves by the late evening of March 19. Broken telephone wires made direct communication from the storm's damage path impossible, but carloads of volunteers moving the injured and dying made it to points north and south of the storm's track to call for more help.

Even before daylight dissipated, men, women and children who were sorting through the wreckage of their homes and businesses stepped on nails, scraped themselves on rusty metal sheets and sought medical care to remove shrapnel from their chests, legs, arms and abdomens. Morphine and anti-tetanus, or "lockjaw" serum, along with clean water, food, clothing and shelter were among the most urgent medical needs in the stricken region.

In Illinois, the request for supplies from Chicago alone included one thousand big army tents; one thousand stoves; four thousand cots, pillows and bed sacks; and twelve thousand blankets, all of which were detailed just to Carbondale.

A lack of records, deeds and other vital statistics hampered the recovery. The tax receipts of the town of Murphysboro were pilfered by the wind and deposited as far as 125 miles away, and scores of people lost their proof of identification, wills, marriage certificates and birth and death records.[92] Paul Cox, a reporter in Robinson, Illinois, published a report detailing the deeds, paychecks, invoices, photographs, rail tickets, letters, postcards, letters and "thousands of bits of paper" he discovered from the region in the days and weeks after the storm in a mammoth lost-and-found effort.[93]

As Red Cross relief workers arrived across the region, the team's goals were consistently in sync when told to reporters and residents: "For every survivor in the storm belt, the same conditions will exist, so far as they can be reproduced by human agencies, that existed before the fury of the elements Wednesday." This goal would be tested to its limits.

People across the country collected whatever they had that they thought might be of some benefit, from shoes to razors and food. The Boy Scouts were put to work in nearby communities, canvassing their home areas for victims and recovering needed supplies that were later distributed by the Salvation Army. Orchestras and theater troupes put on benefit shows to raise funds, including a New York Police Department orchestra show in St. Louis. Sixty cases of blankets weighing more than sixteen thousand pounds were donated by a Nashua, New Hampshire firm. One woman in South Dakota baked forty loaves of bread and sent them aboard relief trains that were passing through. Unfortunately, every loaf spoiled before it could be distributed.[94]

Ten thirty-by-seventy-foot hospital tents were dispatched from Springfield to the region. After arriving, physicians and nurses feared poor sanitation and disease might take more lives than the storm. To cope with the sanitation problem, Dr. Thomas Leonard, the Illinois assistant director of public health, surveyed the area with one sanitary engineer, four nurses and a nurse supervisor, two quarantine officers and four county health superintendents. Together, they brought a field laboratory and as many anti-tetanus and antibiotic medications they could find, but supplies dwindled and areas near Murphysboro completely ran out overnight.

The day after the storm, physicians and medical officers made urgent requests for supplies to regional facilities, and when those ran out, they went to facilities across the country. Red Cross directors in Louisville, Chicago, St. Louis and even points as far away as Cincinnati and New York began receiving calls and messages requesting everything from bandages to vaccines. Late in the evening of March 19, William Fortune, the Red Cross director at Indianapolis, called J.K. Lilly, the president of the Eli Lilly Pharmaceutical Company headquartered there, and initiated a daring scramble for a tetanus vaccine.

With all the available supplies of tetanus vaccine exhausted from St. Louis to Chicago, Lilly called in all the company's available workers for a special night shift to manufacture vials of tetanus vaccine before daybreak. Fortune said the Red Cross directors in Carbondale and Murphysboro, Illinois, were in dire need of the serum. Lilly warned Fortune that because of the serum's short shelf life, without being cooled, there was no way a train could deliver it before it expired. Fortune would have to figure out some faster way of getting it there.

In the early morning hours of March 20, Fortune woke Brigadier General Dwight Altman, the commander of Schoen Field at Fort Benjamin Harrison in Indianapolis. After a cursory "good morning," Fortune got right to the point: "We have 750 vials of tetanus serum. Can you get it to Carbondale?"

Wasting no time, Altman selected two army officers, Lieutenants R.H. Stewart of Indianapolis and Harry Mills of Dayton, Ohio, each a reserve army air force member, to make the airborne delivery.

The two pilots started preparing their planes before daybreak and left Indianapolis at 4:30 a.m., moments after a truck delivered a crate of the life-saving serum. The pilots, they said, expected to reach Carbondale in a little over an hour. There, most of the serum would be left for distribution, and then the pilots would go on to Murphysboro to deliver the rest. The pilots took off under clear, dark skies and landed in a field outside Carbondale in record time. In the span of about ten hours, over two hundred people and two daring pilots willing to fly in the dark initiated the first known medical flight in U.S. history.[95] Another flight piloted by Frank O'Neil left Vincennes, Indiana, on March 21, carrying Sam Guard of the Sears-Roebuck Foundation and newspaper editor E.G. Thiem of Chicago. They conducted one of the nation's first aerial disaster surveys and landed in Carbondale with orders to establish a relief station packed full of clothing, household goods and other supplies from Sears retailers.[96]

On the ground, a regiment of sanitation engineers from Chicago kept watch against disease and began testing the water supplies along southern Illinois, only to find questionable sources of drinking water. The storm had mixed so much debris, coal, oil, chemicals and other hazards into soupy lagoons, reservoirs and water tanks that no water was trustworthy. Large quantities of chlorine and water treatment chemicals were being rushed in from all directions.[97]

Doctors and nurses, thankfully, were in no short supply. So many flooded the area the day following the storm that most returned home in forty-eight hours. After the initial surge of bleeding and traumatic injuries were stabilized, many doctors amicably left the rest to the attention of the remaining area physicians.

Physicians may have stopped the bleeding, but Dr. I.D. Rawlings, a surgeon operating in Murphysboro, put out a request to the U.S. Army,

Relief volunteers and workers arrive in southern Indiana with supplies donated by the Sears-Roebuck Foundation. *Indiana Historical Society, PO551.*

Navy and public health offices for the treatment to stop gangrene, which was beginning to settle in amid the injured survivors with the least-threatening wounds. What initially seemed like minor injuries worsened as surgeons worked on more urgent patients. Dirt in wounds festered over the preceding day and a half to become painful infections. Doctors knew from

World War I that more people would die from gangrene than their initial injuries if they didn't hurry. Gangrene treatment, however, was rarely stocked in most civilian hospitals.

Dr. Thomas Leonard, the assistant director of the U.S. Public Health Agency, told U.S. surgeon general Hugh S. Cumming there were at least 363 surgical cases around Murphysboro, another 305 near West Frankfort and 70 in the Herrin Hospital brought from Bush.

In Washington, Cumming telephoned an order of a gas gangrene antitoxin from Lederle Laboratories in New York, the only manufacturer in the country. Production started immediately, and crates were loaded onto express trains in about a day.[98]

In statehouses in Missouri, Illinois and Indiana, governors and lawmakers near their capitals began hearing wild stories of once-in-a-generation destruction, babies ripped from their mother's arms, schools pulverized and streets red with fire.

Despite knowing the storm's path and that no doubt hundreds—maybe thousands—of people were suffering, William H. Kershner, the adjutant general of Indiana, told reporters the night of the storm that no plans or preparations were being made to send physicians, nurses, medicine or the Indiana National Guard to the region, simply because no official requests for help had been received. Across the Wabash River, Governor Len Small of Illinois ordered troops and the medical corps of the Illinois National Guard to proceed to the devastated area immediately.

In Indianapolis, four hundred telegrams were sent all before midnight on the day of the storm into southern Indiana, mostly from people worried about the safety of their family members and friends in the region. No one knew if the telegraph wires were even reaching their intended destinations. Among the telegraph offices still standing near or in the storm-swept region, a similar number of messages were being sent out to reassure families and ask for help. Operators were overwhelmed and struggled to sort through them quickly. Thus, there were few official channels for local government offices or leaders to make formal requests. If they did send a message—as many county health officers and physicians had—they still had to be sorted and delivered to their intended recipients.[99]

Most telephone and transmission wires were strung along rail lines. The convenience of using the right-of-way made setting up poles and wires easier. Most rail companies used the wires to send messages along the tracks of delays, engine troubles or other issues, so their presence near rail lines helped keep passengers and freight moving. But serious disruptions in communication and transportation occur when a storm moves over the tracks.

The M&O wires were down in Murphysboro; the Southern Railway and C&BI wires were down in Princeton; and the Pennsylvania Railroad lines were down at Chestnut Ridge. More wires were down between Indianapolis and Louisville as the storm front's remnants spawned more tornados near Louisville and in south-central Indiana.

Operators began mapping where they could and could not send messages successfully. Telegrams and telephone calls were being relayed through Chicago in lengthy, circuitous routes around the damaged area. Operators south of the storm's track could contact Evansville, who could contact Louisville, where operators there could relay the message to counterparts near Cincinnati. Operators north of the damaged lines in Illinois and Indiana could relay messages sometimes as far north to Chicago first before a message could be transmitted south to Red Cross or national guard offices in Indianapolis or St. Louis.

Scores of nurses and physicians, however, were not waiting for official requests. Grace Wright, Indiana's federal Red Cross agent, began rushing workers and patients into and out of Princeton, Poseyville and Griffin in taxicabs, ambulances and special relief trains.

Because of the difficulty in transmitting messages, it took three hours to hear from anyone in Owensville, Indiana. Wright learned that the public library in Owensville had become a temporary hospital, and twelve were known to be dead. As news of the damage was tapped or phoned in over the wires, rescue operators learned that Griffin, once a town of four hundred people, was itself "virtually a morgue." Only a part of four buildings out of some two hundred were left standing. The devastation and suffering there seemed impossible to fathom.

President Calvin Coolidge was told of the storm at the White House by aides on the evening of March 18. The morning after the storm, on March 19, condolences from international leaders, including Japanese and Peruvian leaders, themselves dealing with a large fire in Tokyo and a devastating flood in Trujillo, Peru, were sent to Coolidge.

In his role as chief of the American Red Cross, Coolidge encouraged donations and set in motion the "machinery of mercy." The Red Cross was the only official mechanism for large-scale, federal-level disaster relief in 1925. Coolidge, a former Massachusetts governor and vice president, now two years into his presidency after the death of Warren G. Harding, was a thrifty proponent of local government control. He donated $100 to the Red

Cross and encouraged Americans to do the same. He personally believed his presence along the tornado's path "would not accomplish anything" and that it was mere political grandstanding if he did.

The great American tornado was the first of three significant natural disasters to occur during Coolidge's presidency. Two years later, in 1927, the most destructive flood in U.S. history occurred when the banks of the Mississippi River overflowed, killing 500 and impacting some 630,000 people. Later that same year, a November rainstorm flooded Coolidge's native Vermont, destroying 1,285 bridges, killing 84 and obliterating virtually everything in its path. In each situation, Coolidge personally donated money to the Red Cross and refused to get himself or the federal government involved. Property owners, he believed, and state and local governments should bear the costs of recovery.

However, the 1927 floods catalyzed a change in the relationship between the federal government and states. Congress passed a recovery bill later signed by Coolidge that he thought would open "the proverbial floodgates" to federal relief and reconstruction funds.[100] But in the moment of the 1925 tornado, help began arriving within hours of the storm. However, supplies seemingly could not come fast enough or in the proper quantities for those who survived.

At Carbondale the morning after the storm, before the arrival of any relief trains full of doctors and nurses, what few doctors and nurses were there found themselves in a desperate situation, with hospitals jammed, churches and homes filled with the De Soto victims and able-bodied men and children carting the injured on pieces of broken wood, doors, walls or scant bits of fabric and blankets. Any flat surface that could be commissioned as a stretcher had a body on it. The deluge of hundreds of patients and the lack of supplies compelled surgeons to operate without administering any anesthetic.

Operating in the dark and without much equipment beyond their bare hands, rescuers—most of whom were untrained civilians—listened for cries of help and desperately tried to throw water from whatever source was available on open cisterns and fires. In Murphysboro, one reporter noted, "Two dogs exhibited affection for their master by digging at his body, pinned in death under debris of a burning building, despite streams of water played by firemen to drive them off. They stayed until the body was removed."

But among the streams of hundreds of walking wounded, still dazed and confused, women screamed in the most agony at the thought of losing their children. Not knowing what happened or why, children wailed for their mothers and fathers. Between the aisles of bodies in tents, half-destroyed churches and government buildings and schools in outlying areas rested infants, toddlers, children and men and women of all ages. Some were dead, some were alive and many were somewhere in between.

Amid the ceaselessly long line of injured packing into makeshift triage centers, the task of assembling the dead was largely ignored, because there was no time among the needs of those still living. An Associated Press reporter wrote about how the suffering was "enacted amidst scenes of sorrow unparalleled even in these communities to which mining disasters are not unusual."[101] They did not have a name for it then, but post-traumatic stress would smother the survivors and rescuers, some for the rest of their lives. Trying to balance helping the injured, digging for the dead and rescuing potential survivors produced unimaginable stress for the citizen rescuers who, barring any experience in World War I or the Wild West, likely had never experienced anything so significant.

A reporter who witnessed the stream of two hundred dead bodies in Carbondale found the scene "even more pitiful because...even among little children, [scarcely one] had escaped being mangled, scarred or burned— some beyond recognition."

As a gray-haired woman tottered past a row of bodies of schoolchildren who had been killed at De Soto, she seemed to express the sentiments of everyone around her when she turned to a companion and sobbed, "This was no disaster—it was a crucifixion."

The injured told reporters they remembered seeing friends and relatives killed by splinters of wood driven through their bodies. Thousands of children had been separated from their parents, either swept by the winds, caught out in the storm or at school or having lost sight of them.

A three-year-old boy wandered into the West Frankfort City Hall to receive medical care. His broken arm rested in a sling. He was found on the outskirts of West Frankfort, and no one had claimed him yet. Overworked nurses could not understand the toddler when he tried to tell them his name, but he seemed sure his parents were coming for him. None of the nurses or volunteers had the heart to tell him dozens of unknown people were already in the makeshift morgue set up outside.

Working tirelessly into the night, often by candlelight or—if they were lucky—near the headlamps of a car that wasn't overturned, the most any nurse or doctor could usually do was offer a calming word or prayer.

FLOOD IN GRIFFIN

TWO TO SIX DAYS AFTER THE STORM

At the height of the tornado's fury, one man took cover in the railroad station when he saw the tornado cloud and later reported, "As I took a hold of the doorknob, that storm just naturally jerked the station right out of my hand."[102] When Ted McIntire emerged from under the rubble after the tornado struck Griffin, Indiana, he saw "hail as big as goose eggs." Nothing was left standing in the entire town. It was a complete loss. In the immediate aftermath, Griffin joined only Biehle and Gorham as "100 percent destroyed." But the suffering in Griffin would soon take a dramatic turn for the worse.

Piles of splintered timber and collapsed masonry dotted the landscape. The only partially intact structure was a large two-story home owned by a German family just west of where the Griffin School stood. It featured a long porch and several rooms. "Throngs of people stayed there to eat and have a place to sleep until everything could be organized," recalled McIntire years later to meteorologist Peter Felknor.[103] The observance of two other tornadoes circling around the primary tornado near Griffin guaranteed nothing was left in the town. Fifty-four people were killed.

The scores of motoring tourists who came north from Evansville, originally a nuisance to Red Cross relief workers, became messengers as they motored into the outskirts of Griffin. There, they discovered dozens more families living outside their broken homes or plots of farmland west of town. Unable to move far or afraid to leave what meager belongings they had left, survivors gave their names and approximate addresses to passersby, who carried their

A general view of Griffin, with two officers standing amid the debris. *University of Southern Indiana–Rice Library collections.*

information to relief workers in Griffin. Promising to help, most came back on their return trips with food, water and news that help was coming.

In Griffin, relief workers felt confident they were meeting the needs of victims, but as more names of stricken families in rural Posey County came streaming in, Marcus Sonntag, chairman of the Evansville Red Cross who was overseeing operations in Griffin, told volunteers he was considering a request to Indiana governor Ed Jackson to send a unit of guardsmen to help search the countryside for the dead, injured and needy.[104] Jackson took office in January after the Indiana Ku Klux Klan spent $250,000 to get him elected.[105] Unlike government leaders in Missouri and Illinois, Indiana's representatives still were not sending national guard troops to a county until appropriate bureaucratic requests were fulfilled. Like his counterparts in Illinois and Missouri, Governor Jackson began receiving news of the storm the same evening the funnel lifted. He also quietly thanked the governors, executives and heads of state worldwide who sent messages and telegrams filled with condolences and offers to help. And like those of his executive counterparts, his message back to leaders in New York, Pennsylvania, Italy and even Japan was always, "Thank you for your sympathy and kind remarks. The situation is quite in hand. Donations to the Red Cross are most helpful."

Motorists line up for miles to bring supplies, volunteers and sightseers shortly after the storm in Griffin, Indiana. *University of Southern Indiana–Rice Library collections.*

Volunteer women with the Red Cross and other officials pose near a relief headquarters tent in Griffin, Indiana. *University of Southern Indiana–Rice Library collections.*

A train unloads supplies in the distance amid the rubble of Griffin, Indiana. *University of Southern Indiana–Rice Library collections*.

Destruction in Griffin, Indiana, at an unknown location. *University of Southern Indiana–Rice Library collections*.

Damage in Griffin, Indiana. *Evansville-Vanderburgh Public Library.*

Four days after the storm, on March 22, Indiana guardsmen were dispatched to canvass the farmland and hills in the rural portion of the storm's path in southern Indiana. Sensing a need to witness the storm's aftermath, Jackson set out from Indianapolis five days after the storm, on Monday, March 23.

Meanwhile, hundreds of civilian men with saws and hammers and women with clothing, blankets and food came streaming into the tornado's path. The storm was relentless, so they had to be, too. Along with physicians and nurses from Evansville and Indianapolis, they discovered that the area between Princeton and Owensville resembled France's battlefields, with shattered buildings, splintered trees and steel-helmeted guards who had begun maintaining security and enforcing martial law. Fire brigades from nearby towns split up and established perimeters in four quadrants of Griffin, ready to guard against fire.[106]

In the surrounding countryside, picnic parties formed with sightseers—some twenty-five thousand a day by some estimates in southern Indiana alone—sitting with their lunch among the rubble of people's lives until a patrolling trooper encouraged them to move along. Only those with Red Cross passes could proceed in the general direction of Griffin, where, within a day, a crew of twenty-five carpenters began rebuilding homes

Residents and volunteers rest on Griffin's Main Street. The Schultz home can be seen toppled in the background. *Evansville-Vanderburg Public Library*.

The remains of the Griffin School in Griffin, Indiana. *Evansville-Vanderburgh Public Library*.

A dead horse lies among acres of ruin. Dead bodies and livestock posed significant health risks. *Willard Library collections.*

deemed repairable. Seventeen of the men came from Mt. Vernon under the direction of contractors Jacob Behrick and Edward Stallman, who volunteered their services.[107]

For days, carpenters, cooks, physicians, nurses, insurance men and anyone with skills or talent that could be used worked around the clock. Hammers tolled against wood, and the shouts of men digging up debris rang through the night as temperatures cooled in a bleak drizzle to the upper twenties in the countryside.

A long string of survivors who were waiting to be seen by a doctor or sitting under makeshift blankets developed lockjaw, or tetanus. The bacterial infection causes painful muscle contractions in the jaw and neck, rendering a person unable to speak, swallow or move. Dr. Herbert Wagner, the Indianapolis physician working in Griffin, administered antibiotics, and patients recovered quickly. But amid the rain, cool air and mass of people, he was among the first to develop body aches, chills and a fever while working in the outdoor medical tents. After ignoring his own self-diagnosis for days, he was formally diagnosed with the flu and ordered to give up his work for the safety of others.

Newspaper reporters were dealing in precious few facts, but after a day or two, papers were churning out new editions with updates on the dead and the needs of the living. Governor Jackson put out a formal proclamation for donations of money. "I'm confident the people of Indiana will come

A residential area destroyed in Griffin, Indiana. *Evansville-Vanderburgh Public Library*.

Cleanup underway in Griffin, Indiana. *Evansville-Vanderburgh Public Library*.

forward and do their share as they always have," he told one reporter. The Red Cross said money was more important than food or clothing given the current supplies.

But an intense uneasiness settled over the southwest pocket of Indiana. With each newspaper edition came an updated tally of the dead and injured across the Midwest. In some locations, like Murphysboro and Carbondale, estimates were revised down as the weather settled and duplicate names and counts came into alignment. Elsewhere, like in Griffin, the number of dead kept growing.

Further, each newspaper edition was more alarmed by the constant rain and drizzle that fell over the Ohio Valley. Publicly, relief leaders reassured everyone that needs were being met. Privately, hundreds strode to the tops of nearby hills to look out at swelling floodwaters threatening to maroon Griffin and cut off deliveries of supplies and volunteers. "Cheer? There is none. Smile? That is impossible," wrote one reporter in the *Indianapolis Star.* Between the tornado, the fires, the sun festering over the dead and now a looming flood, it seemed the only kind of disaster that hadn't struck Griffin that week was witchcraft.

The same storm system that produced the tri-state tornado on March 18 produced dozens of other tornadoes nationwide, most lasting only minutes.

Remains of Main Street in Griffin, Indiana. *Evansville-Vanderburgh Public Library.*

Debris and damage in Griffin, Indiana. *Willard Library collections.*

Thunderstorms were reported across the Ohio Valley, Midwest, South and plains states into Texas and as far south as Louisiana. That same afternoon, thunderstorms in northern and central Indiana carried intense rain that percolated out of the sky and began seeping downstream into myriad tributaries, creeks and rivers.

Within three days of the storm system, the Wabash River, which empties into the Ohio River, collected millions of gallons of excess stormwater from across the upper two-thirds of Indiana. With ongoing showers and rain along the Ohio River Valley, the Wabash River near Griffin began to rise.

Rescue work under the command of Captain W.C. Hunter and Sergeant George E. Armstrong hastily organized men with shovels, axes and their bare hands to dig under the debris while they still could. The remains of three people were discovered, charred by the fire that had swept out from under the stove at the Kokomoor restaurant—the same restaurant Mary Runyon and her father had observed smoldering from the top of the hill shortly after the tornado.

Beneath the ruins of the George Doll general store, workers unearthed the bones of two unidentified bodies that were likely to remain that way. A third was identified as the remains of ten-year-old Reuben Majors. The death of Reuben brought about a sinking worry among morticians and nurses who thought they had previously identified one body as Majors and buried three days after the storm. Now, the boy who was buried was unknown again. Not wanting to misidentify the remains, investigators

Floodwaters rising a few days after the storm at an unknown location near Griffin, Indiana. *Evansville-Vanderburgh Public Library.*

Men pose near a Red Cross tent and a relief tent in Griffin, Indiana. *Evansville-Vanderburgh Public Library.*

unearthed the casket. It was not long before the unknown boy's grandmother Mrs. George G. Majors recognized the watch that was found near the body and a cuff link, which she said had been gifted to him on his tenth birthday.[108]

Reuben was found near the body of another young child, perhaps a six- or seven-year-old, whom investigators could identify only with a right shoulder blade, three ribs, a left hip and part of a skull. Owing to the body's age and location, it was believed it was all that remained of Chester Price, whose brother Lester Price was also killed in the storm.

The ghastly remains continued to haunt rescuers as a third set of remains was unearthed from the ash heap of the restaurant. They consisted of a skull and a few of the hand bones of an adult. Witnesses nearby recalled seeing a traveling salesman from an Alton, Illinois firm in town at the time of the storm. One witness said he ran into the Kokomoor restaurant when he saw the tornado coming. No one knew his name, and all the bones were so badly burned that they fell apart as workers picked them up. Wilbur F. Smith of the 113th Medical Corps, in charge of camp sanitation, examined the bones and personally aided in extracting them from the ashes and debris. They were turned over to Coroner Sam Davis to be held pending possible identification, a possibility that became increasingly remote.

And still, the workers labored to dig and seek out any sign of life under the direction of Captain Wade S. Hunter of Battery E, 130th Field Artillery, which had been patrolling the district, maintaining order and assisting with operations for days. "They dig," wrote one reporter, "for beneath this mass of debris there comes that awful stench of human flesh. There are more beneath."

Residents persisted, and within five days, on Sunday evening, County Superintendent G. Edward Burns and Chief Attendance Officer Sylvanus Johnson stood together in the one clear street of Griffin, checking over the list of children who had attended the town's school. Griffin students returned to school the next day, March 23. Sitting bleakly at makeshift tables or on the floor, those in attendance were short by thirteen students who did not answer at roll call.[109]

"These thirteen are dead or missing," said Burns, checking their names. "There are others that we haven't heard from, but we will continue to hope that they are being cared for somewhere." Across the region, hundreds of children were being cared for by neighbors or in whatever homes looked suitable for habitation. Sometimes, the children knew the owners of these homes, but sometimes, they were just people from miles away who opened their doors.

Relief workers and residents eating lunch at makeshift tables in Griffin, Indiana. *Evansville-Vanderburgh Public Library*.

"Some of them are still here, living in tents. They will be taken to school at Stewartsville and back by automobile each day," Burns announced. He arranged for students to live in other families' homes in nearby districts, with expenses incurred to be paid by the school district. Red Cross officials began checking lists of families with children to determine which kids were entitled to the meager benefit of living with strangers.

"The others, for the most part, have been taken into the homes of relatives, friends, and others who have generously stepped forward. It is best that they go back at once to the routine of school life. It will help them forget," he added.

The task of bringing order to the confusion of the attendance lists of the storm-swept district in Posey County fell to Truant Officer Johnson. But his strict surveillance of those who missed school loosened up after the storm. Whenever he found a child sitting idly in a shelter or under a tent, he urged them, "For your own good, carry on." Those whose parents needed extra help to reestablish their homes and lives were excused.

Though all the medical and surgical authorities agreed the disease situation was under control, a stream of patients continued to flow into hospitals in Evansville. Mrs. Laura Hedrick; Vernon McIntyre, four; and Chester Cleveland,

thirteen, were sent to the hospital after they were exposed to chilly, damp air–induced pneumonia. Still more were succumbing to tetanus. Reggie Sullivan, eleven, one of the children who was in the school bus that was blown over in the tornado, suffered a severe laceration on his arm and now faced a mounting battle with infection. Doctors believed amputation was the only way to save the boy's life.

Typhoid was another danger, one that had so far been assuaged by maintaining a source of clean drinking water. "Nothing but filtered water is permitted for drinking or cooking," said one nurse. A train car provided by the Illinois Central Railroad to the Red Cross served as a clothing station for workers and the needy, and another was being wheeled in to

Opposite, top: The scene in Griffin after the storm. *Willard Library collections.*

Opposite, bottom: Damage to a home in Griffin, Indiana. *Willard Library collections.*

Above: A young girl rides down a slide in the yard of the damaged Griffin School. *Willard Library collections.*

serve food and water to survivors who could claim whatever they needed—and prepare it themselves.

By the afternoon of March 23, heavy black clouds slung low over Griffin. "They hang as if guardians of the rising waters, which have all but shut the town from the outside world," wrote reporter James Stapp for the *Indianapolis Star*. "Floodwaters tonight are on all sides of the ruins of Griffin. Except for seepage in the fields on three sides, however, the site itself is dry."

Fannie Hodges began the work of sifting through the area surrounding her home. Unlike many homes that were cleanly swept away and revealed nothing but a foundation, Ms. Hodges's home remained standing with four walls, but it had no roof and few possessions inside had escaped being blown away. A Red Cross–issued tent was assembled in her front yard. The tent stood about as tall as her modest home but measured only about nine or ten feet wide. With nothing else to do but pick up the pieces, she sat outside with only the clothes she was wearing, part of a dismantled bathtub and a metal bucket's worth of salvaged belongings. As she sat on a stump alongside her bucket, Rosa Jackson, the wife of Indiana governor Ed Jackson, who was on tour in the area, came to give her a few words of encouragement.

Top: The remnants of a house in Griffin, Indiana. *Willard Library collections*.

Bottom: Destruction of trees and a home in Griffin, Indiana. *Willard Library collections*.

Across town, Shep, a shaggy-coated dog of Claude Schmarr, who had died in the tornado in Griffin, made friends with Governor Jackson during his tour on Sunday. Unsure of what to do with the animal, Arthur Burnett, Schmarr's brother-in-law, asked if the governor would like to adopt the dog. Smiling, Jackson promised to take good care of the dog at the executive mansion in Indianapolis. "And I shall call him Griffin," said the governor.

A day later, John Cowling told a reporter, "I gave Jackson my vote, but I'll be darned if I give him my dog." Cowling, who had lost his Scotch collie, was sure the missing companion was his dog. "If the governor don't believe it's my dog, just let him try to keep him away from me when I yell, 'Here, Frankie!'" Cowling warmly told a reporter.

Governor Jackson made three personal inspections of towns in southern Indiana and drove out of Griffin with his new dog on a highway that crossed the Black River, which was covered with one foot of water. The governor came to inspect the area because he was considering calling a special session of the state legislature to appropriate rehabilitation funds. No such session was ever called.[110]

Jackson's departure was timed with immense luck, as surging floodwaters from the Wabash and Black Rivers surrounded Griffin mere hours after his departure. The waters of the Wabash River at Mount Carmel, Illinois, were at nineteen feet, three feet above flood stage. Griffin sat a mere six miles from the Wabash. The Black River runs east and north of Griffin, and it presented the greatest danger. Having risen five feet in twenty-four hours, its current miraculously shifted thirty feet to the west, saving one bridge over the New Harmony–Griffin Road, which was already underwater. A mile wide and fourteen feet deep, the Bowe River left its banks and sent water over the low-lying areas nearby. Overflowing water was creeping toward the already flooded Wabash River on its way to the Ohio and Mississippi Rivers. For two miles in all directions, only the seats of cultivators and plows abandoned in the fields remained visible above the water.

Residents feared the old bridge over the Bowe River would collapse if debris collected against it. Word from Red Cross officials and hospitals in Terre Haute to the north, Evansville to the South and areas along the White River to the northeast all reported the rivers there were still rising, dispelling any hope those rivers might be able to absorb the rush of water. Levees, too, were at risk of bursting from the mounting pressure. No one knew if the storm had damaged the levees, making them too weak to hold back millions of gallons of flowing water.

Captain Phil Rowe, Battery B, 139th Field Artillery, and George F. Zimmerman, the head Red Cross worker in the area, were so concerned about the danger of flooding that they ordered a full carload of provisions sent into the camps at Griffin for fear the railroad bridges would wash out over the Black River. Motorboats from the larger flood relief boat *Kankakee*, which was docked in Evansville, ferried food, water and medical supplies up the Wabash River and then the Black River into town.

Guards stationed all around town kept a watchful eye on the rising water. Most spent the night turning motorists around after several daring drivers tried to ford the flooded highways and bridges before they stalled in the muddy yellow surge that had burst over the banks. Late in the evening of March 23, the Black River—which itself is more of a stream of sandy strata not usually more than three feet deep—flooded the lowlands on three sides north, south and east of Griffin and completely cut off travel over one road. The water was already axle-deep on the only remaining approach into town from the west, and the waters were still rising at midnight.

Guardsmen and troopers stood over the bridge at the Black River and announced it was still standing, but engineers agreed it was only a matter of hours before it, too, would be washed out. Debris from the storm had swirled into the floodwaters like a great drain, crashing up against the modest stone bridge. Willis Smith, the Posey County road superintendent, worked with a crew of his men and local guardsmen to clear debris, pile sandbags to soften debris blows and unload truckloads of cement blocks to create an artificial levee around the bridge. Telephone linemen tried to raise the single temporary line that was erected after the tornado high enough that it would not fall under water. They all understood that if the bridge went, they would lose their only chance for contact with the outside world, except for the little branch railroad, which ran one modest train a day into the settlement to carry supplies and volunteers in and a few carloads of debris out.

Recalling the 1913 flood that ravaged the region twelve years earlier, fishermen at Webbs Ferry said, "It's only a matter of time before the Wabash backs up into the Bowe and Black Rivers and sends its water over this entire stretch. And when that does, Griffin will go under water."

Naval vessels, small boats and any vessel that could be hauled by State Highway Department vehicles were offered up, ready to sail into Griffin to rescue people from what would become water-soaked, flooded tent cities. The Red Cross worried the most about epidemic diseases that might spread, in addition to the long fight against tetanus that relief workers had already been racing against.

"It is as if fate is playing her trump card," wrote journalist Stapp. The only consolation was that the tracks of the Illinois Central Railroad had been built five feet above the fields on an outstretched berm. As long as the tracks remained dry and passable, slow escape was still possible for the hundreds stranded inside Griffin—if they could get to the train.

Two more crews of men were brought in to drop more sandbags and cement blocks to stave off the water. Like battling a mounting enemy that was marching on their position, soldiers fought to hold the bridge, but despite multiple trucks racing back and forth to New Harmony for cement blocks, the levee was overtaken by the floodwaters. When the bridges and highways finally submerged on Saturday, March 24, Griffin was nearly on its own, and all work to hold the bridges was abandoned.

For survivors, the floodwaters resembled the color of the earth, their skin and their blood. There was nothing left for them to do but watch the water rise. Captain Rowe designated Barrett Station on the Illinois Central Railroad, located two miles east, the new receiving station for supplies destined for Griffin. From there, men would unload supplies by hand onto a motorized hand cart that had been pressed into service by the railroad. Under Rowe's orders, ticket sales on the railroad were forbidden, except on presentation of a pass signed by himself or Red Cross authorities. Train cars stood ready at New Harmony to charge near Griffin to evacuate the town.

Within hours, Captain Rowe ordered his men to use the gas-powered traction car donated by the railroad that could, for now, still traverse along the berm into town. Then, using boats to ferry food, water, medicine and other necessary supplies across the swollen Black River, they would float along flooded streets to deliver goods to waiting trucks or hands on the outskirts of town. It was slow, tedious work that hampered the relief of victims' suffering in prolonged, agonizing ways that survivors in other storm-torn towns did not endure.

Undeterred, an army of guardsmen and volunteers unloaded building materials for a new post office—along with locks and keys for mail—onto a hand cart that men pumped into town around the clock. The sound of hammers and sawing continued as members of the Carpenters Union of Mt. Vernon, Indiana, volunteered to begin erecting homes and structures, even as the obvious risk continued to rise.

The water kept rising. A telephone connected the guards to military headquarters with a single tenuous wire. The high water, they reported, was between the three-mile martial law zone and what was left of Griffin, encircling them like a great moat. Griffin was surrounded and about to go under.

Around 6:00 p.m., Captain Rowe sounded the alarm and ordered all autos out of the outlying areas. Most hurried out while they could. The last car over the bridge was, eerily, a hearse. But dozens remained, unable or unwilling to leave, and they had to be rescued from their vehicles. They then trudged up steep embankments to waiting railcars that whisked them to Evansville. Griffin's former downtown area would not drown, but everyone there would have to wait in near-empty idleness for the water to recede.

RECOVERY

TWO TO FOURTEEN DAYS AFTER THE STORM

Attorney Isaac Levy woke up March 18, kissed his wife, Lillian, and twenty-one-year-old daughter, Constance, goodbye and headed out the door for Jonesboro, located about twenty miles south of Murphysboro, Illinois. He was trying a case in the local court and did not want to be late. The forty-seven-year-old Levy was a lifelong resident of Murphysboro. His law practice, like his character, grew alongside the town's fortunes. He studied law in town, learned everything he could from local attorneys Thomas Phillips and John Herbert and briefly became a state's attorney nine years into his law career. Now, twenty-one years after starting his practice, he was fast becoming a senior member of the Jackson County Bar Association and the Illinois State Bar Association and served on several committees and association boards.[111]

Charming and unassuming, typical of middle-aged midwesterners, Levy held exuded a quiet ambition not bound the geography or size of Murphysboro. For men like Levy, his ambition bubbled over into Murphysboro itself. Ike, as everyone called him, was a prominent and well-respected figure around town, not just because of his legal skills and business acumen, but because the man with a high forehead, ruddy cheeks and distinctive nose held his hometown in such high regard.

After Ike dashed out the door and motored down to Jonesboro, the morning court session sailed by without much distraction until news spread of a storm that had just passed over Murphysboro. Levy jettisoned his remaining court duties and sped back to Murphysboro to find his wife and

NORTH 9TH ST PARK

One of several tent cities. This one was erected in Murphysboro's Ninth Street Park. *Jackson County, Illinois Historical Society collections.*

kids unharmed. But the Murphysboro he returned to that afternoon was nothing like the one he had left that morning.

Flooded with emotions and grief, Levy motored as far into town as he could before the streets became impassable. Everywhere he looked, men, women and children stood in a daze, as if the tornado had left a haze of clouds and destruction in their minds. Setting out on foot, Levy found his wife and daughter near their severely damaged home. It seemed the city was crippled.

Within minutes, groups of men and women began coordinating search-and-rescue efforts. Within hours, physicians and Red Cross relief cars rolled into Murphysboro to administer medication and treatments. Within about two days, citizen committees coordinated rehabilitation and reconstruction, some parcel by parcel and others block by block.

The removal of the debris seemed daunting. Rebuilding vital infrastructure and schools seemed challenging. But unemployment and lack of income seemed to be threats as large as the tornado itself. In Murphysboro alone, some two thousand men were out of work at the Mobile and Ohio Railroad shops. Another three hundred were unemployed from the Brown Shoe Company while it was closed for repair. Hundreds more small business owners and shops were destroyed. Unable to sit idle, they lent a hand to repairs as they joined an army of carpenters, craftsmen, linemen and volunteers who flooded in to hammer their way through the city.[112]

The Mobile and Ohio Railroad shops in Murphysboro, Illinois. *Jackson County, Illinois Historical Society collections.*

The idea of rebuilding seemed obvious to many, but an equal number were not so sure these towns could or should be rebuilt. Residents of De Soto and West Frankfort knew their coal mines—and the reason the town ever boomed—were nearly exhausted. Mines eight to ten miles away were where the jobs went and so, too—logic dictated—went the town.[113]

Most people, however, banished the idea of giving up on their homes. For men like Isaac Levy, rebuilding was an immediate and necessary next step. At an impromptu presentation one afternoon, Charles Ritter, a businessman and one of the wealthiest men in Murphysboro, remarked, "Murphysboro will rebuild." The somber *hurrahs* of hundreds gathered before him echoed around.

Illinois governor Len Small and a dozen relief work officials were nearby, planning a mass funeral that Sunday. Ritter and committee chairmen who were organizing the rebuilding painted the horror of the devastation as they toured the area. But they looked beyond the relief work in what may have been the first much-needed bit of hope and optimism people heard after the storm. "The relief activities," Ritter said, "can be only temporary, it is what will happen after the temporary relief measures that concerns us mostly. The Mobile and Ohio shops are destroyed. The Brown Shoe Company's factory is gone. We must prepare for the future and bring hope to the stricken by assuring them that their jobs will come back."

Top: A public funeral is held on the largely undamaged square in Murphysboro, Illinois. *Jackson County, Illinois Historical Society collections.*

Bottom: The Brown Shoe Company was closed for months following the storm. *Sallie Logan Public Library.*

Ritter continued in his impromptu speech, "The banks of this town are prepared to strain their credit to the utmost to aid its people in restoring their lost homes and industry. We must all be ready to begin work at once. Murphysboro and you will build on its ruins. It may take years to get back to our old status, but Murphysboro will rebuild it."

Ritter, striking with his white hair and ruddy cheeks, climbed down from the speaker's platform with tears in his eyes, and Murphysboro uttered its first cheers since the tornado's arrival three days earlier.

The remains of the Blue Front Hotel after the storm and fires. Men hang on wires to restore service. *Jackson County, Illinois Historical Society collections.*

Rebuilding, it seemed, would require a mammoth infusion of donations and goodwill. The insurance men came shortly after the first wave of doctors and nurses, and then came Red Cross workers and carpenters and craftsmen. Suit-clad representatives from insurance companies had been surveying the damage since early Thursday morning. The assessment of all the larger insurers operating along the storm's track was that less than three-fourths of the storm loss was covered by fire and tornado insurance policies.[114]

In the cities and towns, it was estimated that property was insured for close to three-fourths of its value, especially in the residential districts of towns like West Frankfort, where the homes were mostly built by building and loan company funds. In the mining towns of Annapolis and Leadanna, however, the ramshackle houses that were built, in part, by the mining companies that now faced the decision to rebuild their operations—and people's lives—were deemed worth the expense.

The ratio of insured properties was lowest among the farms and rural communities, where few carried expensive policies. Those who did were insured up to only about 50 percent of their home's value. By April, Illinois Insurance Department investigators were on the ground in southern Illinois after local state representatives and senators witnessed constituents getting less than their fair share of their policies.

Elbert Waller, the Illinois state representative for District 44 and Murphysboro, wrote in an open letter,

> *It has come to my notice, from sources that are credible, that some insurance adjusters, under guise of prompt and easy settlements, are driving rather hard bargains. Ruins to the disadvantage of those who lost property in the recent storm and are perhaps now accepting help in the manner that they never had to before in their lives. I have asked the Insurance Department of Springfield to send an investigator to see that the interests of the people are protected. Such representative is now on the ground.*

He went on to encourage residents to speak to lawyers in Jackson County, whom all pledged to give free advice in any matter surrounding the storm.

Isaac Levy was among those attorneys advising people on how to navigate their insurance policies. The tornado's track had failed to break the region's ties. Even if most people in the rural farmland were uninsured, their farms bought and sold food, livestock, feed, farm equipment and supplies that were built, packaged and sold in the cities. Their fortunes and futures were inextricably linked.

A relief tent set up by the Red Cross serves as a headquarters for the county in the center of Annapolis, Missouri. *Annapolis, MO: Centennial publication, Iron County, Missouri Historical Society, 1971.*

After a few days, the general situation was deemed well in hand with the needed quota of doctors and nurses to attend to some seven hundred injured in and around the town. The graver problem of providing semipermanent housing, food and clothing for the helpless thousands who had been herded together was most pressing. Residents whose homes were unharmed or mostly unharmed on the outskirts of town opened their doors and packed in two, three and sometimes as many as seven families.

Thousands of residents were living in tents, but more were needed. Each tent was furnished with blankets and makeshift bedding supplies. Thousands more tents arrived by the trainload in Murphysboro. Another six thousand tents arrived in Carbondale on March 22, and coordinators there began planning to build a tent city in an area deemed suitable by sanitation engineers for preventing disease.

Some five hundred families were resting each night in Pullman sleeper cars near Murphysboro. Hundreds more crammed into the sleeper cars at serviceable railyards along the storm's path. The Illinois Central and Mobile and Ohio Railroads began offering free passage to anywhere in the United States to all storm refugees, providing some hope for those with family elsewhere in the country. For others, abandoning the area was an exercise in protecting their mental health.

Within five days of the storm, long-distance telephone service had been restored in Murphysboro, and outlying areas were also receiving repairs. Post offices had been repaired or rebuilt to ensure people could send and receive mail, even if they no longer owned a mailbox.

News came from as far away as Chicago that hospitals were offering limited free treatment for children injured in the storm. Even after a week of rescue operations, bodies and survivors were still being unearthed. Rescuers at the Logan Elementary School were surprised to find a young boy under tons of debris and masonry. The twelve-year-old surfaced to see light and fresh air for the first time in three days. He seemed dazed and confused but quickly ran away in a frightened tear for his mother.

More volunteers from unions and trades around the country came to offer their help and support in any way they knew how. Perhaps no group did more in the aftermath than the National Funeral Directors Association (NFDA). Joseph Sletten organized a grave registration service in Murphysboro, along with his counterparts in dozens of other locations across the storm's path. In Illinois, a radio appeal on KYW Chicago from Harry Kilpatrick, secretary of the Illinois State Association of the National Funeral Directors Association, asked all state members to render assistance. With the help of guardsmen

Top: A guard stands watch at an intersection near a residential area in Murphysboro, Illinois. *Sallie Logan Public Library*.

Bottom: A tent city is erected in Murphysboro's Logan Park. *Sallie Logan Public Library*.

who were still maintaining security, Mr. Sletten organized embalmers, grave diggers and morticians across the area to identify and record the victims' names as best they could.

The most chilling unidentified cases were frequently those of children and babies, some of whom were assumed to have been blown in from other towns by the wind. Many NFDA members embalmed and buried the dead at cost or at no charge to the families to keep disease under control. In a remarkable feat of organization and paperwork, nearly every victim who could be identified, even those buried in mass graves, received an individual grave marker.

Flowers sent by florists across the country piled up at memorial sites and in new, large cemeteries. Despite there being significant work to do elsewhere, men labored for days to reset grave markers that had been blown over in the storm. Chunks of gravestones that were hit with debris were carefully collected in hopes of restoring them. Proving the storm did not just impact the living, many old trees in cemeteries and graveyards across the region had been toppled, ripping their roots and nearby caskets out of the ground. These caskets had to be sawed free and reburied.

Money continued to pour into the Red Cross, $100 from the tiny town of Oxford, Michigan; $500 from Muncie, Indiana; $1,437.05 from the Wabash Shop Employee Association; $10,000 organized by the *Courier-Press* of Evansville, Indiana, $500 of which came from the Graham Brothers Truck Company. Kiwanis, Lions and Rotary clubs across the country set goals of $1,000, $2,500 or even $5,000 and more. They quickly met their goals and set about to do it all again.[115] Unions sent volunteers and cash, all directed to the Red Cross.[116] The combined efforts of 168 chambers of commerce in Illinois and 6 state federations of the American Farm Bureau, American Red Cross, American Legion, Salvation Army and numerous other smaller agencies in civic and fraternal bodies united to raise more than $1.5 million, or about $17 billion in 2024.

The donations were counted county by county. Hundreds of dollars in rural counties and thousands from urban areas were wired or hand-delivered along with other supplies. Across the country, individuals, churches and service organizations, like Rotary Clubs and Moose Lodges, heard the appeals of their sister organizations across Missouri, Illinois and Indiana. A frenzy of people captivated by stories from the storm packed carloads of supplies into trains headed for the relief efforts. Cars packed with shoes, clothes, blankets and even perishable foods, like pies, were loaded up and moved in.

So swiftly had the railroads swung into service, most stations in the storm's path were receiving two or more deliveries of supplies a day. Highways were cleared of debris, and the main streets in Murphysboro and elsewhere were passable about two days after the storm. The St. Louis Red Cross, which was coordinating efforts in Missouri and helping with some efforts in southwest Illinois, reminded people to stay off the roads, however, as "every available highway [is] taxed to capacity in caring for the injured and homeless." The roads were also congested with funeral processions.

Traffic was heavy on the highways and roads across the entire stretch of the storm's path, many vehicles waving flags or bearing placards reading "funeral." Police and military officers were strict in issuing passes for these processions. Still, so many hundreds of relatives and friends came to mourn and bury their loved ones that funeral processions could not be denied. A string of automobiles hundreds of vehicles deep stretched over the highways through Benton, West Frankfort and Annapolis. At Parish, Illinois, where Mine no. 18 was destroyed, crowds were large, creating traffic where there was never traffic.

The task of mourning loomed large over everyone. The voices of clergymen broke through the air all day Friday, Saturday and Sunday after the storm. On Friday, March 21, the day was quiet, with a bright sun and soft wind blowing over mourners at Saint Andrews Cemetery, where six clergymen could be heard reciting prayers and services at once.

Overall-clad gravediggers near Murphysboro rotated between shoveling earth and serving as pallbearers. One after another, their friends' and neighbors' mangled, bruised and warped bodies came into stark view. Some, like Frank Keough, J.G. Andrews and Ernest Henchliffe, who survived the storm, only to be burned alive in the Mobile and Ohio Railroad shops, were identifiable only by their watches.

At Tower Grove Cemetery in Murphysboro, Bill Mullinhall survived the storm by taking refuge in the cemetery's large iron vault. He looked out the vault's tiny window slit and watched Murphysboro blow away all around him. "It's one of the weird things of life that I should have found shelter from the cyclone where a lot of those killed in it will rest," he said.

S.J. Howell, who had been driving ambulances around southern Illinois for twenty-six consecutive hours, finally found a moment to rest on Friday. Lying down on a casket in one of the morgues, Howell shut his eyes and immediately fell asleep on the flat wooden lid. A short while later, a tearful woman touched his arm and said, "Is this one of the bodies also?" Mr. Howell immediately awoke and reassured the onlookers he was very much alive.[117]

14

REBUILDING

ONE TO THREE WEEKS AFTER THE STORM

History was made twice in one week. First came the tornado itself, which was already known to be the worst tornado in U.S. history and the worst weather disaster since the great Ohio River flood of 1913. Then came the recovery efforts to feed, clothe and shelter the survivors in the Red Cross's largest relief effort on record.[118]

In the storm's immediate aftermath, the myth many locals believed about Murphysboro being immune from cyclones because they sat in a valley was shattered. Illinois governor Len Small and members of his staff traveled south from Springfield to Murphysboro, Gorham and several other towns in the damage path on March 19. One observer said they found "a shambles of wreckage, unprepared for all" that was happening around them. A week later, on March 26, the governor and his staff returned, only to be "astounded at the miracle."[119]

To the surprise and delight of officials, everyone was housed, clothed and fed. Water supplies were safe in most areas, and boil advisories were canceled. Carpenters were at work rebuilding, and indeed, it seemed all enmities, jealousies and political lines were cleanly swept away as everyone worked together to rebuild the lives of their neighbors. The organizational capacity and "cool-headed direction" of each community were, they deemed, to credit.

Governor Small "cut through the reins of restraint," as one official put it. This meant Illinois leaders brushed aside their political concerns of government overreach and got down to work. "Illinois tries to be a big mother," said one official who toured Murphysboro on the condition of anonymity. That it all appeared to be going so smoothly was described as a "miracle." It seemed even more miraculous compared to the slow, bureaucratic response in neighboring Indiana, where guardsmen and state aid ran aground against formal requests and the chain of command.

Local Lions Club district governor Wayne Townley met with members of the West Frankfort and Murphysboro Lions Club, which had been established only two months prior with a total of twenty-six members, and told the local school boards to order new textbooks and supplies for every child at an estimated cost of $10,000. Lions Club International would cover the entire cost. In most towns, including Murphysboro, schools were reopening within the week and would meet in churches that had survived the storm until their buildings could be rebuilt. Even efforts to save trees that were stripped of bark or uprooted in the storm were made. Dr. O.B. Ormsby, president of the Murphysboro Park Board, commissioned a group of men and arborists to see how they could preserve the mature trees in the town's parks and streets.

Another $500,000 was quickly earmarked for distribution by an Illinois state relief fund. Public schools, town halls and public buildings that

A FREAK OF THE STORM. TWO VIEWS OF A TREE AT HINCHCLIFFES, 22ND AND EDITH. MURPHYSBORO. WHERE A BOARD WAS DRIVEN THROUGH THE TRUNK OF A TREE LIKE AN ARROW AND A PIECE OF A SHINGLE WAS THEN DRIVEN THROUGH THE BOARD.

Two guardsmen inspect a board that was driven through a tree and a shingle that was driven through the board in Murphysboro, Illinois. *Jackson County, Illinois Historical Society collections.*

were uninsured or underinsured were placed at the front of the line for reconstruction funds under the direction of Isaac Levy. Isaac "Ike" Levy, the Murphysboro attorney who was out of town at trial the morning of the storm, was fast becoming one of the town's heroes. Levy was named general chairman of the relief committee and Red Cross Advisory Committee. It was Levy who led the charge to disburse money to individuals and families. Under his stewardship, the Red Cross distributed tens of thousands of dollars to thousands of families and encouraged a "Rebuild Murphysboro" pledge drive. With the help of the local newspaper, residents pledged to rebuild their homes or businesses "as good or better" than they had been on the "Builder's Band Wagon."

Levy used his experience with the law to author a bill in the Illinois legislature that provided $275,000 to rebuild the devastated schools in Jackson County. Prior to the storm, Levy and fellow members of the county bar association had petitioned state and local leaders to build a new courthouse. The old one was deemed antiquated, small and increasingly something of an eyesore. Perhaps using the storm damage as further reason for rebuilding, Levy drafted the resolution presented to the Jackson County Board of Supervisors for a new courthouse, which was completed in 1928 and still stands.[120]

Despite commitments from the railroad shops, Brown Shoe Company and others to rebuild, men were still out of work. Mr. Levy originated the idea and promoted paving the road from Murphysboro to De Soto and from De Soto to Hurst.

The road, which was more of a dirt path that suffered from ruts, washouts and gummy mud that made travel in the spring and winter nearly impossible, was the perfect opportunity to both improve the area and put men to work while their employers rebuilt. Mr. Levy traveled to Springfield for dinner with the governor, a meeting, the paper noted, that lasted nearly until midnight on March 31. The local labor plan impressed Governor Small, who was also impressed with the local attorney turned relief chairman's candid detail. The governor told him to get to work "right now." The Illinois legislature had already authorized the use of $500,000 (about $8 billion in 2024) to rebuild.[121] Mr. Levy triumphantly told a reporter from the *Daily Independent*, "The state is going to take care of us down here."

Governor Small had already traveled to the region and seen the devastation, but even a week after the storm, Mr. Levy's testimony and powerful belief in the power of the "Egypt" region of southern Illinois made a lasting impact. After he returned home in the middle of the night, Mr.

Levy got to work organizing rolls of workmen and outlining the needs for the construction project and other necessities in the area. When the Mobile and Ohio Railroad Company began to consider moving its operations elsewhere in the aftermath of the storm, it was Levy and others of his committee who helped the Illinois Senate pass a resolution that urged the company to make an "immediate decision…to rebuild its shops at Murphysboro." Levy was determined to make Murphysboro rise again.

In most towns, a committee of business and government leaders decided when, to whom and how much money was distributed. Each had "unlimited power to act."[122] Red Cross organizations were receiving equally large amounts of money. In St. Louis, $80,000 had been collected; in Chicago, $1 million; and millions more from across the country were all allocated for rebuilding.

Not everyone felt the same miraculous camaraderie and outpouring of support espoused from out-of-towners. In a joint letter from Jackson County sheriff C.E. White, Murphysboro chief of police Joe Boston and Major Robert Davis, the three lawmen pleaded with people to protect against rape. "Men of all character [are] swarming in for anything they might find to do that is unlawful or mean." The officials asked that parents keep young girls off the streets after 7:00 p.m. unless they were safely escorted.

Amid the fear of crime and rape, residents questioned if this was the time for them to move. Hundreds of demoralized refugees in the tornado's path decided it was time to leave and put up "for sale" signs on their lots. Distressed at the notion, local newspaper and businessmen branded them "calamity howlers" and declared it nothing but "unpopular grapevine stories." For the most part, crime was relatively tame, and the fear was likely overblown in the imaginations of people already in distress.

William Baxter Jr., the assistant to the vice-chairman of the National Red Cross, arrived in Murphysboro from the St. Louis office on April 1 and reminded residents, "Murphysboro was not built in a day, and it will not be rebuilt in a day." Among praise for residents' heroism and hard work along the storm path were small reminders that months—perhaps years—of work remained ahead. "Such heroism makes me keenly sensitive to the great responsibility resting on the Red Cross," Baxter said.

Sizable public and private funds helped business districts and industry. State legislatures and banks lent money and conducted public works projects. But to help individual and family needs for money, the Red Cross established a system to meet, survey and study each family. Trained family workers in each district met with families and individuals, usually at the tents pitched where their homes once stood. An accounting of each family's size, prior assets, cash on hand, insurance policies and needs were documented. Men who had lost their jobs due to the collapse of their mine, railroad shop or business were awarded more money than those who still had jobs. Those with more children received more than those who had fewer. Storm-related medical and funeral bills were also accounted for. Armed with this information, a clipboard and a pen, Red Cross family workers made recommendations for rebuilding homes and refurnishing them with clothes, food and other necessities. Officials were quick to point out that the Red Cross "does not give any help that is not needed" and that "it does not help a family that has sufficient income to meet its losses."

For thousands of victims, however, the difference between "sufficient," "what they had" and "what was not needed" was up for interpretation. Garrett Crews detailed to meteorologist Peter Felknor years later, "The Red Cross gave my father $1,500 toward the cost of rebuilding. I don't know what the total cost was, but I would imagine it was about $2,500. I do know that without this help my father could not have rebuilt."

Nearly everyone on the outskirts of the tornado's path suffered the loss of some or all of their roofs and virtually all of their windows. Red Cross workers distributed rolls of roofing material, some donated by lumber and construction companies, to patch the holes. Still, with supplies short and glass virtually impossible to find, people tacked blankets, sheets or wood debris over their windows to keep the wind and rain out. These people were not homeless but felt very nearly so with little chance of receiving a recovery check against those who had lost everything.

The Salvation Army worked in tandem with the Red Cross to distribute food after the storm. Milk depots were established in De Soto, Bush, Hurst and Murphysboro, Illinois, as well as in points in Indiana, where mothers could receive milk for their young babies. Hundreds of mothers lined up for bottles. Fracture specialists were brought in to help set bones. Chlorine was added to drinking wells. Lids for garbage pails were disbursed, and a garbage collection schedule was established amid a seemingly never-ending pile of trash. The Red Cross also announced funds to encourage builders to establish sewer connections when rebuilding homes and businesses, even in cases where there was no sewer connection before. These measures, everyone believed, would make the region healthier than it was before.

In the day-to-day lives of many, however, receiving a garbage pail and a bottle of milk with some blankets and a makeshift tent was not enough. In a 2022 interview, Jane Sims recalled the story of Joe West, who used to laugh at his aunt, who survived "flying through the air in a bathtub and landing in a tree" outside Murphysboro. But when he remembered the suffering of others, he became much more serious about the failure of the relief work. Stories abounded about "the guy who had nothing left but a hole in the ground, and all he ever got was a doughnut." Unlike the Salvation Army, the Red Cross sometimes sent a bill afterward for food and some supplies—including their issued bucket and blankets—if it was believed those who received it could have afforded it.

In the small and mid-size towns affected by the storm, everyone had a general sense of their needs, their neighbor's needs and where everyone started before the storm. Wealthy business owners, mine operators, bankers and other professionals may have strained under new and old debts but were generally no worse for wear after a few years. Middle-class families, however, struggled against being too poor to rebuild and too wealthy to receive relief funds. The Red Cross family workers who judged some to be poor and others wealthy enough to recover mostly or entirely on their own soured many people's opinions on the recovery for a lifetime. For hundreds of middle-class laborers and business owners, their recovery was entirely stunted by the realization they were on their own for thousands of dollars' worth of repairs and new and old debts.

The situation was often more dire for farmers who had lost their mules, horses and farm animals. Even if the Red Cross family workers cut them a check for some of the loss and insurance covered some other small percentage, their remaining losses were likely still too much to recover their livestock, hay or crops, fields, tractors, feed and supplies—and certainly not within the planting and growing season. Hundreds of farmers lost loved ones, money and time. The most fortunate farmers were those who had rare insurance policies that covered crop losses or whose mules survived so they could be put back to work. State Farm Bureau field offices organized large field cleanup days to help clear fields with the help of as many as thirty-six tractors at once.[123]

Hundreds more farmers, professionals and laborers faced a reality in which they still owed a mortgage on a plot of land and a house that no longer existed in addition to new debts for rebuilding and no way to farm or work for a way to pay for any of it. They were left to scratch at the land with whatever they had left in hopes the earth would yield a surplus.

There were still winners among the many losers of the frustrating Red Cross relief lottery. People whose livelihoods before the storm were too poor to maintain what they had and who often lived with few supplies, little food,

The Indiana Farm Bureau relief tent, similar to many found along the tornado's damage path. *Indiana Historical Society, PO551.*

leaky roofs and deteriorating houses came out of the storm with what was surely believed to be a clean start. To a person living in a ramshackle house with little income and several kids, family social workers judged them to be in no position to pay to rebuild, so they got significantly higher proportions of the relief funds, often living in better housing and with more new clothes after the storm than they had before.

Homeowners struggled with insurance companies denying their claims, even when they had coverage. If a house was blown apart and then burned, the insurance claimed the damage was from wind and not fire or vice versa—whichever was not covered. Windstorm insurance, as it was known, became a popular product after the storm for those who could afford it. New companies, like the Murphysboro Mutual County First Insurance Co., advertised it was now ready to underwrite policies exclusively for farmers.[124]

A supply of new tractors to tend and clear fields arrives from the Indiana Farm Bureau in Griffin, Indiana. *Indiana Historical Society, PO551.*

For almost everyone of average means, however, community support was all they had to rely on. Lost and found notices littered local newspapers for weeks afterward. Lost rings, photographs, documents and even rugs and appliances appeared in places as close as next door and as far away as one hundred or more miles. The Kraus and Son Hardware store lost its delivery book. The Clark farm lost a light red cow. A report card for a Murphysboro student was found 150 miles away in the backyard of an Indiana family.[125] The recovery of these documents, heirlooms and possessions was cause for celebration and relief.

One of Standard Oil's employees, Hugh Williams, was killed in the storm. He was driving his work truck on Walnut Street when a falling telegraph pole struck him in the chest. Perhaps as a result—or perhaps out of moral responsibility—nine local employees of Standard Oil had the most miraculous windfall when it was announced the company would give each of them $1,725 in cash, not as a loan but as immediate relief. Standard Oil further donated $7,200 (about $123,000 in 2024) to the region's relief funds and several trucks, gas, oil and workers in the surrounding area to help.

The Murphysboro Paving Brick Company resumed operations on April 2. The company had not suffered much damage from the storm but had been without power since the tornado struck. Some 125 men worked at the brick plant, a pillar of the industrial community of the region. It was also one of the largest contributors to railroad freight for the Mobile and Ohio Railroad. Since most train loads were measured and priced by the ton, resuming operations of heavy bricks meant the local railroad could continue to support its operations.

Still others took the opportunity to improve their lots. Henry Borgsmiller Sr., a veteran wholesaler in Murphysboro, took the opportunity to fully realize his dream of rebuilding his operations with a freight car switch outside his door. Borgsmiller was described as a "pioneer citizen and merchant…considered one of the best-informed men in town on property valuations and futures." With his vote of confidence on the future of Murphysboro, others followed, including Fred Roberts's Dodge dealership, the Able Cleaning and Dyeing Co., the Wisely Flower Store and S.B. McNeill and Sons, a large bakery operation at Sixteenth and Walnut Streets, next to the Borgsmiller property. New and rebuilt apartments, hotels, milling operations, stores and homes were all sprouting up around Sixteenth and Seventeenth Streets for blocks in every direction.[126]

On the outskirts of downtown Murphysboro, even homes and businesses that were not damaged or destroyed by the storm got in on the improvement bandwagon. Mary Van Cloostere, who owned and operated a store at Walnut and Tenth Streets, spent $20,000 to rebuild and modernize a series of her buildings. The First Lutheran Church, which had long thought about building a new church at Fourteenth and Manning Streets on land it had already purchased, decided to make the move, since its prior church had been destroyed. Likewise, the Christian church at Ninth and Hanzen Streets rebuilt at Fifteenth and Pine Streets.

MOVING ON

ONE TO THREE MONTHS AFTER THE STORM

A month after the storm, frustrations over rebuilding efforts left many middle-class families feeling angry and shut out. Perhaps their largest source of frustration was the Mobile and Ohio Railroad, with its lack of commitment to rebuilding a railyard and shop in Murphysboro. With some mines closing operations after the storm, laying off fifty or one hundred men here and there, the mounting unemployment numbers began to worry residents. First, news came that a new Mobile and Ohio operation in Jackson, Tennessee, was being eyed by company executives. Money, residents believed, was being diverted from Murphysboro to Tennessee.[127]

By April 10, the St. Louis–based M&O had reassured local leaders that a new facility for building cars, a roundhouse and a mechanical shop would be constructed in Murphysboro. M&O vice-president Norris told Isaac Levy and local state representatives, "The local shops will practically be replaced in ninety days." Within that time, the railroad expected all but 60 or 75 men of the original 650 shop employees to be rehired. "We consider Murphysboro a most important working point and the logical work headquarters north of the river," he said. "We have enjoyed a nice business here."

Satisfied with the promise, an April 10 *Murphysboro Daily Independent* report declared industry was "coming back big." It wrote, in part, "The Brown Shoe Company, within three months' time, hopes to have its 509 local workers housed in a more modern plant, here, prepared to better meet the heavy demands. The plant had been fighting year after year for more room. Now, it is coming back with electric elevators to do away with the cumbersome wooden stairways. Concrete may replace certain areas of hardwood floors."

"Isco-Butz Silica Company is coming back by leaps and bounds with a new future ahead of it on the east side," wrote another report. The storm had wrecked the company's boiler room walls. Intensive work was assured at the Egyptian Iron Works, too. The Southern Illinois mill began churning again, as did the promise of the Reliance Milling Co., which was being rebuilt. In each case, all the mills' and ironworks' fortunes were partly tied to the railroad.

By the end of April, workers' and Murphysboro leaders' outlooks on the M&O had improved. The construction of a ten-stall roundhouse maintenance facility for train engines was underway to replace the prior thirteen-stall roundhouse. While some worried about the reduction of three stalls, M&O Railroad vice-president Norris assured the public the new stalls would be larger, capable of holding more in fewer stalls. They were to be one hundred feet long, compared to the prior stalls, which were forty feet long. The number of linear feet of track would be twice as much as before, up to one thousand feet.[128]

More new facilities at the railyard would be constructed of all-new steel. Designed to be fireproof, the new sawmill and mechanical buildings would double as facilities for the constructions of train cars, which would bring a new line of work for local laborers.

But two weeks later, on Friday, April 24, one thousand men and women went to a meeting at the Hippodrome Theater to hear the demands of former M&O shopmen: "Stop awarding building contracts to anyone not shipping via the Mobile and Ohio Railroad."[129]

Unlike most boycotts, in which people insist on withholding money or services from a company until it complies, shopmen were worried the railroad, which had yet to finish rebuilding and restoring its $745,000 annual payroll, might not think the city was a profitable, sustainable business venture anymore.

Tons of lumber, brick, masonry, concrete, sand, gravel, fill dirt, steel, nails and other building supplies were funneling through the storm-wracked region every day, almost all over competing rail lines. The Red Cross relief committees, local chambers of commerce and dozens of other agencies, unions and tradesmen were spending millions of dollars in donations, government funds and relief grants. Merchants and builders, however, either in pursuit of a good deal or more profit, recognized they could stretch their dollars for supplies brought in on cheaper railroad operations.

In 1925, railroads charged by weight, and lines with deeper pockets could squeeze rivals out of business by undercharging against competitors long enough to bankrupt them. Then out of spite or greed, they could raise rates afterward and behave as monopolies. In Murphysboro, two rival rail lines likely saw an opportunity to undercut a long-established competitor that had invested thirty-seven years of work in the area and saw it wiped clean in a matter of minutes.

But out of fifty loads of building material that had arrived in Murphysboro alone since the storm, only two were shipped over the M&O. T.S. Edgell, an M&O employee, said at the meeting twenty-three carloads of building material were delivered so far in the rebuilding effort, and none were from the M&O. Some $4,025 was spent transporting the material, which, he said, "would employee 35 M&O men for a period of 30 days."

At the meeting, Elmer Stephens, a former employee in the mechanical department at the M&O turned chairman of the meeting, invited comments from the crowd. "We're asking everything and giving nothing in return," said local merchant and former mayor Josiah Davis. John Keough, another merchant, characterized the situation as "not only unfair but dangerous as well."

Murphysboro Chamber of Commerce secretary Henry Burch appeared before the crowd to represent the chamber. "The Red Cross is here doing splendid work," he told everyone standing shoulder to shoulder. "That this and other relief organizations are intensively and mercifully active here are, for the time of the emergency, temporary. But the Mobile and Ohio Shops is the hand that fed and clothed permanently, year after year." Former mayor Davis recalled how the M&O had been the primary industrial operation in Murphysboro since he was a boy. "I have a standing order with my company to ship over the M&O."

A resolution was proposed to great cheers, and it read like the resolution the Illinois legislature had passed nearly a month earlier, which called for the reconstruction of the line's operations. This resolution called for merchants and homebuilders to utilize the line more frequently in rebuilding. By May 29, a familiar sound rang across town in the form of the whistle at the M&O shops. "It always sounded good. It always meant much," wrote one reporter.[130]

As new materials came in, all the old ones needed to be removed. Across towns and farmland, fires burned bright in the daylight as pillars of thick, black smoke rose into the air under close observation by local fire marshals. The job of cleaning up debris posed obvious challenges, like how to sort through it, where to take it and how to move it. After property owners were satisfied they had recovered all they could from their homes or businesses,

it was decided that burning the remnants was the fastest, cheapest way to manage the wreckage.

In Murphysboro, entire lots and blocks were set aflame after bulldozers pushed nearby debris away to create a firewall. Fire Chief Herring and Illinois state fire marshal Chamber supervised the burning of half a block at Twenty-First and Elm Streets. Crews at Seventeenth and Walnut Streets were working their way west, shoveling debris into piles to be burned and then cleared away for new construction. Many property owners stood a short distance from their lots, watching it and everything that had been swept in get burned away, as if it was some form of therapeutic memorial. Others cried as what remained of their homes—and often their last remaining dollar—vanished into ash and smoke. The Longfellow School, essentially destroyed by the tornado, was demolished and set ablaze. It later became a city park and the home field of the Murphysboro Clarkes baseball team. Today, a plaque can be found there in honor of those children and teachers killed during the storm.[131]

A mere $10,000 in public funds had initially been allocated in Illinois for cleanup work. Even less was administered in Missouri and Indiana. With so much debris to sift through, crews began warning residents not to use the

Top: A panorama view of Spruce Street taken in 1926, one year after the storm, shows the recovery in Murphysboro, Illinois. *Sallie Logan Public Library*.

Bottom: A panorama view of Spruce Street taken just after the storm in Murphysboro, Illinois. *Sallie Logan Public Library*.

freshly cleaned lots as storage for debris. No one could decide where to put all the splintered lumber and warped steel. After Director Herring discovered that several cleaned lots in Murphysboro had been refilled with great stacks of wreckage and sometimes equally grand piles of clothes, bedding and other materials, he signed off on a plan that would prohibit cleaning off the lots of anyone who was found moving wreckage onto a newly cleaned lot. "Stringent reprisals must be taken, or the cleanup never will be completed," he said. Doubling back, teams lit everything on fire again and bulldozed the ashes into waiting trucks bound for landfills.

Local governments were responsible for picking up the pieces and the bill for cleanup. An Illinois state auditor's report in May 1925 showed many counties and towns in the storm's path were deeply in debt. Murphysboro was $169,078.63 in debt, and the amount was likely to increase over the following year.[132]

Still, it seemed everyone was carrying on as if there were no imaginable alternative. The Brown Shoe Company announced it was nearly done rebuilding and would resume work on June 1, 1925. About four hundred workers were to report back to a new facility with new machines and equipment. Another one hundred workers were to be called back as rebuilding was finished. Called a "marvel of reconstruction," the plant had been left as nothing more than unsheathed stacks of floors surrounded by collapsed brick walls with no roof. The new plant was airier, more spacious and included more natural light from windows than the old one. New chain-driven systems and safety features to prevent fires and injuries were in place.[133] At an open house on Memorial Day, May 30, seventy-three days after the storm, hundreds wandered through the plant to experience one of the first fully rebuilt factories in town. Delightful rumors swirled that company leaders were not going to allow the storm to delay their annual company picnic that summer either.

Two other signs of life carrying on emerged when county assessors appeared on their annual rounds to survey properties for tax collections. In most localities, the law assessed properties as they were on April 1 that tax year. For many, this meant they had nothing more than a broken-down house, an empty lot or a mere tent. It was decided in most localities that citizens could opt to pay their previous year's assessment or whatever the valuation of their damaged lot was for that year. Much to Jackson County treasurer Art Lawder's surprise, taxes were being paid faster than there were in most previous years and on their original valuations. Knowing they needed to support their communities, people lined up to pay their full, normal tax amounts.

A makeshift new library was opened at the Murphysboro Chamber of Commerce—the first for the county. *Their Yesterdays*, by Harold Bell Wright, was the first book chosen by a patron on loan for two weeks. Books by Sinclair Lewis, Shakespeare and encyclopedias were donated to the library in so-called book showers by women's clubs and readers across the country. Other popular books included in the library were *How to Reduce and How to Gain*, *The Mother and Her Child*, *Worry and Nervousness* and *How to Feed the Baby*, by Dr. William Sadler. Plans for a permanent library building were underway.

In another sign that life was returning to normal, political factions began to splinter over the return of former Williamson County sheriff George Galligan. He had been exiled by Klan-controlled leaders and the local board of supervisors after a local Klan raider, S.G. Young, and Deputy Sheriff Ora Thompson shot each other to death in a shootout. Now, anti-Klan candidates had been swept into power in that May's election. A new board of supervisors, a new mayor and a new chief of police in Herrin sat firmly against the Klan. Sheriff Galligan's return caused no ruckus this time in Springfield or Governor Small's office, despite the agreement made between all parties that he would never return to Herrin.

Communities made remarkable recoveries physically, but the personal and financial strains would last a generation. In a small cemetery outside De Soto, survivors buried thirty of the town's children and forty more adults out of a population of five hundred on March 21.[134] Sixty-five gravediggers worked endlessly at the cemetery, which swelled to hold one hundred new mounds. Grave sites everywhere bared fresh dirt amid damaged trees. Women stood with tears streaming down their faces amid sobbing children as men remained too busy digging to mourn. Only between intermittent funerals—usually nothing more than reading the person's name, if it was known, and a brief prayer—did they stop digging. Each grave was marked with a wooden cross that included a name scrawled in pencil.[135]

A hearse, sometimes unaccompanied and sometimes followed by a small procession, would enter the cemetery before hurrying away to the next victim. The process was so rapid that no one stopped to grieve or notice how bleak the cemeteries appeared for weeks.

Boxes of flowers from Chicago were carefully sorted into seventy-one small sprays by the loving hands of women and young girls in De Soto and elsewhere, who explained, "We have no flowers, and we do not want to miss anyone." A government airplane circled De Soto and its cemetery three times, dipping gracefully as it swung over the open graves to drop flowers. It exemplified to the mourners the sympathy the nation extended to them. In nearby fields, horses and a few cattle, representing, in some instances, everything the victims had left, peacefully grazed amid the debris while volunteers picked up detritus so plowing could begin.

Then as soon as a flower was placed and a prayer was said, people would raise their heads and return to what was left of their homes, as one mother who left a little bow in the De Soto Cemetery expressed it, "to begin life again."

EPILOGUE

CONTEMPORARY ANALYSIS

T he final death and injury count was officially set months after the storm. It took time for coroners to ascertain the victims' causes of death and allow the injured to recover or perish. The real number would not be fully realized until January 3, 1926, when Gervae Bervis, a West Frankfort, Illinois miner, became the last known person to die from his injuries sustained in the storm.

The supercell storm and tornado traveled 219 miles through three states, leaving its path of destruction and death in three and a half hours. In its wake, it left 13 people dead in Missouri, 541 in Illinois and 76 in Indiana. The seriously injured included 103 in Missouri, 1,130 in Illinois and 401 in Indiana.[136] Ultimately, 695 people were killed either directly or indirectly by the storm, and at the very least, 1,634 were seriously injured. There were thousands more with minor injuries who were never formally seen for extensive treatment. The storm system that carried this long-lasting funnel spawned multiple other tornadoes in five states in places as far away as Littleville, Alabama; Holland, Kentucky; and Gallatin, Tennessee.[137]

The April 1925 issue of the *Red Cross Courier*, the agency's official monthly publication, devoted five pages to the storm's recovery and relief work, mostly for victims of the single tri-state tornado. The agency spoke briefly about the storm, writing, "In sheer destruction of life and property, the tornado matched a modern battlefield. It was the greatest single domestic disaster to call for the services of the Red Cross since the San Francisco fire of 1906 and the Ohio Valley flood of 1913. More than 800 persons were killed and some 3,000 injured."[138] As a reporter for the Murphysboro *Daily Independent* observed, "The Red Cross account erred only in that it says the roar of the storm warned man and beast. There was no roar. There was no warning in Murphysboro. The tornado literally sneaked upon them. Houses began falling by the time citizens realized a terrible storm was upon them." Indeed, the weather forecast in many papers that morning said merely, "Rain probable tonight and Wednesday. Colder Wednesday or Wednesday night."

Forecasting the storm was not part of any official agency or government department—but not for want of trying. In 1882, the U.S. Army Signal Corps, the first U.S. government agency charged with forecasting, tried to identify what caused tornadoes. Segreant John P. Finley was charged with determining how tornadoes formed and whether they could be predicted. Finley identified fifteen rules for early tornado forecasting after observing a significant tornado outbreak in 1884. His rules included the presence of a low-pressure area, high temperature gradients, increasing humidity from the southeast, the time of year and wind velocities.

Published in the 1888 *American Meteorological Journal*, Sergeant Finley's rules made keen observations about the ingredients necessary for tornado formation. His thirteenth rule also noted: "Tornadoes frequently occur in groups with parallel paths, within a few miles of each other."[139]

Still, tornado forecasting was nearly impossible with any accuracy. Since areas believed to be prone to tornadoes were so large in any given forecast, the chances a person would not see a tornado remained high and could also cause people to lose faith in the warnings. The U.S. Army Signal Corps established a ban on using the word *tornado* for fear it would incite panic among residents. In 1887, the report of the chief signal officer noted, "It is believed that the harm done by such a prediction would eventually be greater than that which results from the tornado itself." The ban on the word *tornado* lasted until the eventual creation of the civilian National Weather Bureau in 1890 and into 1950, even after U.S. Air Weather Service meteorologists issued the first tornado warnings in Oklahoma. The Weather Bureau became the National Weather Service in 1970.

Many still tried to forecast tornadoes, however. Farmers instinctively sensed storms based on premonitions of doom, angry tell-tale skies, temperature changes and the reactions of livestock and birds. The tri-state tornado was different. It seemingly gave off no sound, probably due to the wind pattern and lack of solid objects around it. It gave off no smell and no inkling it was coming until it was on top of people.

Within a day of the storm's wreckage, three National Weather Bureau meteorologists set out to survey the storm's path. Clarence Root was dispatched from the Weather Bureau office in Springfield, Illinois, along with William Baron of the Cairo, Illinois office. Albert Brand of Evansville drove north to survey the Indiana portion.

For seven days, Root and Baron traversed "as close to the storm track as roads would permit." Their report, published in the March 1925 *Climatological Data: Illinois Section*, records the extensive damage. They concluded, "It can positively be stated that there was only one tornado in Illinois and that it was continuous from Missouri to beyond Princeton, Indiana."[140]

Like today's meteorologists, Root and Baron looked for a debris path, the direction in which trees or poles were bent and the presence of ground scouring where the grass and low-level brush may have been ripped or torn out of the earth in a visible twisting pattern. Green grass and ferns turned brown almost instantly as they received a week's worth of abuse in mere seconds, leaving a distinctive brown trail.

Without being able to fly over the area, Root and Baron made visual assessments from the ground and, admittedly, without surveying every inch of the path, made quick observations in rural areas too far from roads or rail lines to travel by automobile. With so much devastation, there was no way they could hike into the backcountry of Missouri.

Scientists in 1925 also lacked definitive ways to measure wind. The most common method for measuring a storm's windspeed came from measuring the distance rail cars were blown from their tracks. Since tracks were easily identifiable—even if a tornado removed the iron rails from the ground—and train cars had consistent and quantifiable weights, researchers could deduce the wind speed in an area where a car was toppled over or thrown. The tri-state tornado toppled centuries-old trees, ripped up tracks and blew train cars several dozen yards. The wind speed at the base of the tri-state tornado was more than two hundred miles per hour, placing it firmly within the strongest EF5 rating, which has been used by the National Weather Service since 2007.

Root told a reporter in Carmi, Illinois, he estimated the velocity of the tornado "was 60 miles an hour, and that of the whirling tornado about 400 miles an hour."[141] Root was correct about the sixty-mile-per-hour progression. Based on timing reports, the twister moved at an average speed of sixty-two miles per hour. It peaked at seventy-three miles per hour near the Illinois-Indiana border, ranking it among the fastest in addition to the deadliest and longest tornadoes in U.S. history. But four-hundred-mile-per-hour wind estimates were too high. Contemporary meteorologists know even the strongest tornadoes rated as EF5 on the Enhanced Fujita scale usually produce only EF5-level damage across a relatively small portion of their damage paths, with EF4-level damage surrounding it.

The tri-state tornado was likely an F5-level storm with brief peak winds around 300 miles per hour along some of the path, primarily in Illinois, and average F4-level winds around 200 to 250 miles per hour along most of its extraordinarily long track. Under the modern Enhanced Fujita scale, the tornado was likely an EF5-level storm for much of its Illinois track and an EF4-level storm along its early and late stages in Missouri and Indiana. Winds over 318 miles per hour would rate the tornado an off-the-charts F6 on the prior Fujita scale, a distinction Dr. Tetsuya Theodore Fujita labeled as "inconceivable." This rating does not exist on the EF scale, simply because anything above 250 miles per hour is thoroughly destructive.

The tri-state tornado of 1925 remains the deadliest in United States history, partly because of its remarkable duration. But it is not the deadliest in the world. That distinction is held by the April 26, 1989 Saturia-Manikganj tornado that passed through Bangladesh. At F4 strength, it killed over 1,300 people, injured 12,000 and left 8,000 homeless across fifty miles.[142] Bangladesh experiences tornadoes regularly, and its dense population centers make for dangerous targets.

Contemporary weather science also knows with certainty what Sergeant John Finley identified during the Civil War: "Tornadoes frequently occur in groups with parallel paths, within a few miles of each other." A detailed analysis published in the May 4, 2013 *E-Journal of Severe Storms Meteorology* by Robert H. Johns, Donald W. Burgess, Charles A. Doswell III, Matthew S. Gilmore, John A. Hart and Steven F. Piltz gives the potential that at least some of the storm's track involved different tornadoes.[143]

Eyewitness accounts near De Soto, Illinois, and the Illinois-Indiana border account for two or three concurrent satellite funnels visible from the ground. The Johns report plotted damage points and eyewitness accounts to speculate, "Path segments at the beginning of the potential damage path in eastern Shannon County, MO, and at the end of the potential path in central Pike County, IN, were both likely from separate tornadoes." The May 4, 2013 report goes on to say,

In the very rural and hilly terrain of southeast Missouri, there were areas with a minimum of human development and no known witnesses to the tornado (parts of Reynolds, Iron and Madison Counties). This led to

several relatively long damage path gaps >3.2 km (2 mi). The existence of relatively long gaps prevents confidence in the continuity of the first section of the path. Beginning in central Madison County, MO, and continuing to Pike County, IN, a distance of 280 km (174 mi), there are no gaps >3.2 km (2 mi), more strongly suggesting that the tornado was likely continuous for that path segment. Because of having the highest density of damage reports and the most eyewitness reports, the part of the main damage path that is 243 km (151 mi) long from central Bollinger County, MO to the west edge of Pike County, IN can be considered likely a continuous path.

The National Weather Service continues to use original assessments from Root and Baron to conclude the storm's path was 219 miles long. The Johns report suggests it was, at minimum, 151 miles long and, at most, certainly 174 miles long. The truth of the remaining 45 miles is lost to history. We will never know with absolute certainty how long the storm's path was. It is also possible the tornado was on the ground a few miles before Ellington, Missouri, and that its path exceeded 225 miles.

But even with conservative measurements, the tri-state tornado of 1925 holds numerous records, including being the deadliest tornadic death event for schools. One-third of all the storm's victims were children. Murphysboro and De Soto suffered the worst losses. Smaller schools in rural White County, Illinois, and several others in eastern Illinois and Indiana that were vacant at the time of the storm were all destroyed. In a rare fit of good news, the principal at the little Parrish, Illinois School had noticed the storm on the horizon, locked the doors and kept the students inside; 90 percent of Parrish was destroyed, but the school was among the 10 percent spared.[144]

The Johns report mentions a previously unreported tornado that struck rural Washington and Jackson Counties the same night of the tri-state tornado. "[The] path and trajectory suggests that it may also have been produced by the same supercell. This new tornado started about 75 minutes later and about 105 km (65 mi) east-northeast of the apparent end of the Tri-State tornado damage path in Pike County, Indiana."

That remnant funnel struck the north side of Washington County, Indiana, where, according to a report in the *Salem Democrat*, the storm "started its work of destruction at the home of Tal Lockwood, on the north pike. Every building on the place was badly damaged and some completely destroyed except a wash house near the dwelling. It was near this place than an automobile, belonging to a Mr. Hamilton, of Medora, was blown from the side of the road and carried down the hillside into a ravine below where it was demolished." A few other homes and barns, including Mont Baker's house and barn, were destroyed. Baker's wife and daughter were injured after being caught under the wreckage. Baker had a hard fight to save his wife before fire destroyed what was left of his home.[145]

The significance of the storm is undisputed, and its track and duration were incredibly long, even using the most conservative of estimates. A second analysis by Robert A. Maddox in the *E-Journal of Severe Storms Meteorology*, published in 2001, noted the thunderstorm that originally spawned the tornado was "not unusually intense." In fact, there appears to have been "no outstanding aspects of the meteorological setting that would explain the extreme character of the Tri-State Tornado." The report notes, "As the supercell and dryline moved rapidly eastward, the northward movement of the warm front kept the tornadic supercell within a very favorable storm environment for several hours. Apparently, this consistent time and space concatenation of the supercell, the warm front, and the dryline for more than three hours was extremely unusual."[146]

Midwesterners who were accustomed to seeing tornadoes were unprepared for a storm of this magnitude, precisely because they could not recognize it until it was on top of them. Like hurricanes, tornadoes also have "eyes." But unlike hurricane eyes, in which people on the ground can experience several calm minutes under clear blue skies, the people inside a tornado's vortex get mere seconds. People caught in the tornado's two-mile-wide base routinely described a "three-gust sensation." One man in Gorham, Illinois, described it as a "whoosh, puff, and whoosh."

Survivors who were not killed by debris felt the wind outflow from one side of the funnel that pushed air down. Then, once the initial outer wall of the funnel passed over them, a powerful pressure difference lifted everything and everyone inside the eye as if it was lifting them for the rapture. Certainly, many people may have believed it was the end times and that God was calling them upward to the heavens. But just as they felt the upward-lifting sensation, the back side of the funnel passed over them and forced them down again.

Contemporary meteorologists do not know with certainty what amount of force and air pressure is necessary to produce a tornado; they know only when the ingredients are present.[147] In Iron County, Missouri, on March 18, 1925, the temperature difference, wind speed, atmospheric pressure and moisture mixed to produce a cool and warm air boundary that began to tumble and maintain these ingredients for three and a half hours.

The tri-state tornado held epic grandeur in the memories of those who survived it a century ago. It has faded from most people's memory today, as it blew many of the era's institutions, documents and memories into oblivion.

In the hours following the storm, there was hardly any noise or light except the shadowy glow of fires. Amid partly cloudy skies, the moon rose higher over the remnants of seemingly inessential structures that had been blown away, shining a chilling light over what once flowered and mattered in people's lives. The region's vanished trees, shops and farmsteads showed that, for a moment, nature let loose while Midwesterners held their breath. Amid the near-complete disintegration of the social fabric in the hours after the storm, the region and the nation rallied.

The wonder of nature's fury and force stretched so far across the land that most people failed to grasp it, even during and after the storm. Recognizing people had the technology to communicate long distances, the precursors to tornado spotter networks appeared, helping alert neighboring communities that a tornado was coming. It's believed these networks were the start of a downward trend in tornado death tolls that extends to this day.[148]

The tri-state tornado of 1925 changed attitudes. It challenged prevailing wisdom and notions about the weather and united communities. After the funnel receded back into the clouds, the dark fields of the land rolled on, just as life rolled on for those who survived. Tomorrow, they vowed, they would strive to rebuild and stretch out faster, ceaselessly beating back against the force of the wind.

NOTES

Chapter 1

1. Cli-Mate: MRCC Application Tools Environment, Midwestern, "Daily Values at ARCADIA."
2. Ancestry, "Samuel Marion Flowers."
3. Maddox, Gilmore, Doswell, Johns, Crisp, Burgess, Hart and Piltz, "Meteorological Analyses," 1–27.
4. Govinfo, "Report of the Chief."
5. U.S. Census Bureau, "1920 U.S. Census Report."
6. *Ellington Press*, March 19, 1925.
7. "Public Notice," *Ellington Press*.
8. *Ellington Press*, March 19, 1925.
9. U.S. Department of Commerce NOAA-NWS, "Weather Ingredients."
10. *Ellington Press*, March 26, 1925.

Chapter 2

11. McGee, "1925, Missouri Annual Reports."
12. Ibid.
13. *Wayne County Journal and the Piedmont Weekly Banner*, April 23, 1925.
14. *Pittsburgh Press*, March 19, 1925.
15. Forrest, "Tornado!"
16. Find a Grave, "Osero Kelley."
17. *Pittsburgh Press*, March 19, 1925.

18. *Maryville Daily Forum*, March 20, 1925.
19. *Kansas City Star*, March 19, 1925.
20. *Poplar Bluff Republican*, March 19, 1925.
21. *Greenville Sun*, March 19, 1925.
22. "4,000 Killed and Injured," *Poplar Bluff Republican*.
23. *St. Louis Post-Dispatch*, March 18, 1925.
24. "Storm Destroyed Entire Village," *St. Louis Star and Times*.
25. *Poplar Bluff Republican*, March 19, 1925.
26. *Greenville Sun*, March 19, 1925.
27. "Cyclone Victims Panic Stricken," *St. Louis Globe-Democrat*.
28. "Windstorm Wednesday Takes Death Toll," *Dexter Statesman*.

Chapter 3

29. "Obituary," *Daily Independent*.
30. "Gorham Woman Describes," *Alton Evening Telegraph*.
31. "East Side School, Power Plant Partly Wrecked," *Daily Independent*.
32. "Elkville," *Daily Independent*.

Chapter 4

33. FundingUniverse, "Brown Shoe Company."
34. Testa, "Spirit of Historic Murphysboro Schools."
35. "7-Year-Old 'Sinner,'" *Philadelphia Inquirer*.
36. Sims interview.
37. "'Baldy' Storm Cradle," *Daily Independent*.
38. "823 Dead, 2,990 Hurt," *McHenry Plaindealer*.
39. "Storm Toll," *Daily Independent*.
40. "Storm Victims in St. Andrews," *Daily Independent*.
41. "Memorial Day," *Daily Independent*.
42. "Eye-Witness Describes," *Marion Evening Post*.

Chapter 5

43. Edmonds, "George N. Albon Sr."
44. *Portrait and Biographical Record*, 786.

45. "Graeff Dies Tuesday," *Daily Independent*.
46. "Rabble Rouser," *Evening Star*.
47. "Hundreds Laid to Rest," *Philadelphia Inquirer*.
48. Ibid.
49. Levins, "Author Recounts."
50. Hottensen, "Survivors Remember."
51. *Poplar Bluff Republican*, March 19, 1925.
52. Ibid.
53. *Maryville Daily Forum*, March 20, 1925.

Chapter 6

54. City of West Frankfort, "Local History"; Summers, "West Frankfort Coal Mine Disaster."
55. *St. Louis Post-Dispatch*, March 21, 1925.
56. *Evansville Courier*, March 23, 1925.
57. *Maryville Daily Forum*, March 20, 1925.
58. *St. Louis Post-Dispatch*, March 21, 1925.
59. "Eye-Witness Describes," *Marion Evening Post*.
60. Ibid.
61. *Fresno Bee*, March 21, 1925.
62. *Indianapolis Star*, March 23, 1925.
63. "Hundreds Laid to Rest," *Philadelphia Inquirer*.

Chapter 7

64. Thomas, "Griffin Tornado."
65. *Indianapolis Star*, March 26, 1925.

Chapter 8

66. "Local Man," *Indianapolis Star*.
67. *Star Press*, March 22, 1925.
68. "Latest Tornado Death List," *Star Press*.
69. "Survivors of Storm Swept Country," *Evansville Journal*.
70. *Star Press*, March 22, 1925.

71. Lashley interview.
72. U.S. Department of Commerce NOAA-NWS, "Startling Statistics."

Chapter 9

73. *Indianapolis Star*, March 19, 1925.
74. Cosmos Mariner of Cape Canaveral, "Tri-State Tornado."
75. *Indianapolis Star*, March 19, 1925.
76. *Fresno Bee*, March 21, 1925.
77. "First Estimates of Fatalities," *Chattanooga Daily Times*.
78. Anderson, "Dr. Herbert Theodore Wagner"; Ancestry, "Helen Fawcett Wagner."
79. *Indianapolis Star*, March 23, 1925.

Chapter 10

80. Library and Archives Canada, "Personnel Record FWW Item."
81. Bishop, "Magnificent Seven."
82. Stationery Office, "Supplement."
83. *Daily Independent*, April 3, 1925.
84. "Obituary," *Daily Independent*.
85. *Indianapolis Star*, March 24, 1925.
86. "Local Man," *Indianapolis Star*.
87. "Go Get 'Em," *Daily Independent*.
88. *St. Louis Post-Dispatch*, March 21, 1925.
89. *Indianapolis Star*, March 23, 1925.
90. "Strange Sense of Humor," *Evening Star*.
91. *Indianapolis Star*, March 23, 1925.

Chapter 11

92. "Cyclone's Sense of Humor," *Buffalo Courier*.
93. "Storm Wafted Papers," *Daily Independent*.
94. "Chaos Gives Way," *Evansville Courier*.
95. *Wichita Eagle*, March 20, 1925.
96. *Carmi Tribune-Times*, March 26, 1925.

97. "Hundreds Laid to Rest," *Philadelphia Inquirer*.
98. Ibid.
99. "Local Man," *Indianapolis Star*.
100. Wallace, "Address."
101. *Baltimore Sun*, March 20, 1925.

Chapter 12

102. Sutton and Sutton, *Nature on the Rampage*, 85.
103. Felknor, *Tri-State Tornado*, 4, 32, 58, 80.
104. *Rushville Republican*, March 21, 1925.
105. Egan, *Fever in the Heartland*, 282.
106. "Flood Waters," *Muncie Evening Press*.
107. "Floods Subside," *Evansville Press*.
108. *Indianapolis Star*, March 24, 1925.
109. "Flood Waters Isolate," *Evansville Courier*.
110. Foughty, "Brief History of Special Sessions."

Chapter 13

111. Ancestry, "Isaac K. Levy."
112. *Fresno Bee*, March 21, 1925.
113. *Indianapolis Star*, March 23, 1925.
114. "Hundreds Laid to Rest," *Philadelphia Inquirer*.
115. "Wabash Workers Gifts," *Herald and Review*.
116. *Evansville Courier*, March 23, 1925.
117. "Hundreds Laid to Rest," *Philadelphia Inquirer*.

Chapter 14

118. "Go Get 'Em," *Daily Independent*.
119. "Storm Toll in Schools," *Daily Independent*.
120. Duncan, "Isaac K 'Ike' Levy."
121. *McHenry Plaindealer*, March 26, 1925.
122. *Daily Independent*, March 25, 1925.
123. *Princeton Daily Clarion*, May 12, 1925.

124. *Daily Independent*, April 21, 1925.
125. *Daily Independent*, April 15, 1925.
126. *Daily Independent*, April 18, 1925.

Chapter 15

127. "Murphysboro, M. & Shops Assured," *Daily Independent*.
128. "All Steel Saw Mill," *Daily Independent*.
129. "Shopmen Demand Shipment," *Daily Independent*.
130. "Long May She Blow!" *Daily Independent*.
131. Testa, "Spirit of Historic Murphysboro Schools."
132. "Indebtedness," *Daily Independent*.
133. "Shoe Factory Will Resume," *Daily Independent*.
134. "Hundreds Laid to Rest," *Philadelphia Inquirer*.
135. *Indianapolis Star*, March 23, 1925.

Epilogue

136. U.S. Department of Commerce NOAA-NWS, "Startling Statistics."
137. "First Estimates of Fatalities," *Chattanooga Daily Times*.
138. National Archives, "*Red Cross Courier*."
139. U.S. Department of Commerce NOAA-NWS, "NOAA 200th Feature Story."
140. Geelhart, "Tri-State Tornado of 1925."
141. *Carmi Tribune-Times*, March 26, 1925.
142. *Encyclopaedia Britannica*. "Saturia–Manikganj Sadar Tornado."
143. Johns, Burgess, Doswell, Gilmore, Hart and Piltz, "1925 Tri-State Tornado Damage Path," 1–17.
144. Fliege, *Tales and Trails*, 191.
145. *Salem Democrat*, March 25, 1925, 1.
146. Maddox, Gilmore, Doswell, Johns, Crisp, Burgess, Hart and Piltz, "Meteorological Analyses," 1–27.
147. Lashley interview.
148. Doswell, Moller and Brooks, "Storm Spotting," 544–57.

BIBLIOGRAPHY

Alton Evening Telegraph. "Gorham Woman Describes How Tornado Struck." March 20, 1925. Newspapers.com. https://www.newspapers.com/image/17255028/.

Ancestry. "Helen Fawcett Wagner 1889–1963." Find a Grave. https://www.ancestry.com/discoveryui-content/view/22787229:60525.

———. "Isaac K. Levy 1878–1963." Find a Grave. https://www.ancestry.com/discoveryui-content/view/56522425:60525?tid=&pid=&queryId=2c8c9db664d94ed474aebc1e7ca2d552&_phsrc=CLT1&_phstart=successSource.

———. "Samuel Marion Flowers 1876–1925." Find a Grave. https://www.ancestry.com/discoveryui-content/view/101567024:60525.

Anderson, John C. "Dr. Herbert Theodore Wagner (1886–1935)." Find a Grave. December 27, 2009. https://www.findagrave.com/memorial/46040119/herbert-theodore-wagner.

Baltimore Sun. March 20, 1925. Newspapers.com. https://www.newspapers.com/image/373416613/.

Bishop, Arthur. "The Magnificent Seven: Part 12 of 18." *Legion Magazine*, November 1, 2005. https://legionmagazine.com/the-magnificent-seven/.

Buffalo Courier. "A Cyclone's Sense of Humor." April 26, 1925. Newspapers.com. https://www.newspapers.com/image/410278784/.

Carmi Tribune-Times. March 26, 1925.

Chattanooga Daily Times. "First Estimates of Fatalities None Too High; Storm's Dead 823." March 20, 1925. Newspapers.com. https://www.newspapers.com/image/604071217/.

City of West Frankfort. "Local History: West Frankfort, Illinois—A Record of Perseverance." https://www.westfrankfort-il.com/local-history.

Cli-Mate: MRCC Application Tools Environment. "Daily Values at ARCADIA (MO) USC00230224." Midwestern Regional Climate Center. https://mrcc.purdue.edu/CLIMATE/welcome.jsp.

Cosmos Mariner of Cape Canaveral. "Tri-State Tornado—March 18, 1925." Historical Marker Database. January 20, 2022. https://www.hmdb.org/m.asp?m=190734.

Daily Independent. March 25, 1925. Newspapers.com. https://www.newspapers.com/image/11984038/.

———. April 3, 1925. Newspapers.com. https://www.newspapers.com/image/11986654/.

———. April 15, 1925. Newspapers.com. https://www.newspapers.com/image/11989475/.

———. April 18, 1925. Newspapers.com. https://www.newspapers.com/image/11990331/.

———. April 21, 1925. Newspapers.com. https://www.newspapers.com/image/11990823/.

———. "All Steel Saw Mill for New M'Boro Shops." April 21, 1925. Newspapers.com. https://www.newspapers.com/image/11990668/.

———. "Andrew Graeff Dies Tuesday, Aged 80 Years." January 7, 1925. Newspapers.com. https://www.newspapers.com/image/11967378/.

———. "'Baldy' Storm Cradle Was a Fifty-Tonner." April 3, 1925. Newspapers.com. https://www.newspapers.com/image/11986419/.

———. "East Side School, Power Plant Partly Wrecked by Storm." August 18, 1925. Newspapers.com. https://www.newspapers.com/image/11541176/.

———. "Elkville." March 27, 1925. Newspapers.com. https://www.newspapers.com/image/11984967/.

———. "Go Get 'Em." April 1, 1925. Newspapers.com. https://www.newspapers.com/image/11985925/.

———. "Indebtedness of Counties and Cities." May 13, 1925. Newspapers.com. https://www.newspapers.com/image/11515386/.

———. "Long May She Blow!" May 29, 1925. Newspapers.com. https://www.newspapers.com/image/11520288/.

———. "Memorial Day to Remember Pupils Killed." April 23, 1925. Newspapers.com. https://www.newspapers.com/image/11510692/.

———. "Murphysboro, M. & Shops Assured, Facing Biggest Work Boon in History." April 10, 1925. Newspapers.com. https://www.newspapers.com/image/11988205/.

———. "Obituary." March 30, 1925. Newspapers.com. https://www.
newspapers.com/image/11985571/.

———. "Shoe Factory Will Resume on June First." May 22, 1925.
Newspapers.com. https://www.newspapers.com/image/11518273/.

———. "Shopmen Demand Shipment via M. & O. Lines." April
25, 1925. Newspapers.com. https://www.newspapers.com/
image/11511283/.

———. "Storm Toll in Schools Reaches 19." March 26, 1925.
Newspapers.com. https://www.newspapers.com/image/11984097/.

———. "Storm Victims in St. Andrews; the Injuries." March 31, 1925.
Newspapers.com. https://www.newspapers.com/image/11985680/.

———. "Storm Wafted Papers Listed at Robinson." March 31, 1925.

Dexter Statesman. "Windstorm Wednesday Takes Death Toll in Three
States." March 20, 1925. Newspapers.com. https://www.newspapers.
com/image/581065325/.

Doswell, Charles A., Alan R. Moller and Harold E. Brooks. "Storm
Spotting and Public Awareness since the First Tornado Forecasts of
1948." *Weather and Forecasting* 14, no. 4 (August 1999): 544–57. https://
doi.org/10.1175/1520-0434(1999)014<0544:SSAPAS>2.0.CO;2.

Duncan, Laura Whistle Cates. "Isaac K. 'Ike' Levy (1878–1963)."
Find a Grave. February 13, 2013. https://www.findagrave.com/
memorial/105104777/isaac-k-levy.

Edmonds, Mary. "George N. Albon Sr. (1858–1951)." Find a Grave.
February 21, 2009. https://www.findagrave.com/memorial/34044257/
george-n-albon.

Egan, Timothy. *A Fever in the Heartland: The Ku Klux Klan's Plot to Take Over
America, and the Woman Who Stopped Them*. New York: Penguin Random
House, 2023.

Ellington Press. March 19, 1925. Newspapers.com. https://www.newspapers.
com/image/491452349/.

———. March 26, 1925. Newspapers.com. https://www.newspapers.
com/image/491452371/.

Encyclopedia Britannica. "Saturia–Manikganj Sadar Tornado." April 19,
2023. https://www.britannica.com/event/Saturia-Manikganj-Sadar-
tornado.

Evansville Courier. March 23, 1925. Newspapers.com. https://www.
newspapers.com/image/767543072/.

———. "Chaos Gives Way to Organized Relief." March 21, 1925.
Newspapers.com. https://www.newspapers.com/image/767542816/.

———. "Flood Waters Isolate Griffin Area." March 23, 1925.

Evansville Journal. "Survivors of Storm Swept Country Recall Incidents of Tornado." March 22, 1925. Newspapers.com. https://www.newspapers.com/image/772739342/.

Evansville Press. "Floods Subside in Tornado Zone." March 23, 1925. Newspapers.com. https://www.newspapers.com/image/763653124/.

Evening Star. "The Rabble Rouser." April 26, 1925. Newspapers.com. https://www.newspapers.com/image/618302819/.

———. "Strange Sense of Humor Shown by Tornado in the Middle West." April 26, 1925.

Felknor, Peter S. *The Tri-State Tornado: The Story of America's Greatest Tornado Disaster*. Bloomington, IN: iUniverse, 2004.

Find a Grave. "Osero Kelley (1891–1925)." October 28, 2011. https://www.findagrave.com/memorial/79410083/osero-kelley.

Fliege, Stu. *Tales and Trails of Illinois*. Champaign: University of Illinois Press, 2003.

Forrest, Kent. "Tornado! The Cyclone at Annapolis—26 November 1925." May 22, 2010. https://www.ancestry.com/mediaui-viewer/tree/2548298/person/-1442786955/media/ecd7bdd0-07d6-4d04-bcfa-2a269b482c32?_phsrc=Acb1&_phstart=successSource.

Foughty, Trevor. "A Brief History of Special Sessions in Indiana." Capitol & Washington. March 19, 2018. https://web.archive.org/web/20200420231407/https://www.capitolandwashington.com/blog/2018/03/19/a-brief-history-of-special-sessions-in-indiana/.

Fresno Bee. March 21, 1925. Newspapers.com. https://www.newspapers.com/image/700816998/.

FundingUniverse. "History of Brown Shoe Company, Inc." http://www.fundinguniverse.com/company-histories/brown-shoe-company-inc-history/.

Geelhart, Chris. "The Tri-State Tornado of 1925." National Weather Service Heritage—Virtual Lab. U.S. Department of Commerce NOAA-NWS. https://vlab.noaa.gov/web/nws-heritage/-/the-tri-state-tornado-of-1925.

Govinfo. "Report of the Chief of the Weather Bureau 1925–26." https://www.govinfo.gov/metadata/pkg/SERIALSET-08779_00_00-002-0529-0000/mods.xml.

Greenville Sun. March 19, 1925. Newspapers.com. https://www.newspapers.com/image/589468549/.

Herald and Review. "Wabash Workers Gifts to Storm Victims $1,437." March 28, 1925. Newspapers.com. https://www.newspapers.com/image/90651449/.

Hottensen, Chris. "Survivors Remember Tri-State Tornado 90 Years Later." *Southern Illinoisan*, March 22, 2015. https://thesouthern.com/news/local/surivors remember-tri-state-tornado-90-years-later/article_aaa494e1-8cce-5d12-bd92-b8638fe33056.html.

Indianapolis Star. March 19, 1925. Newspapers.com. https://www.newspapers.com/image/104828066/.

———. March 23, 1925. Newspapers.com. https://www.newspapers.com/image/104833778/.

———. March 24, 1925. Newspapers.com. https://www.newspapers.com/image/104834265/.

———. March 26, 1925. Newspapers.com. https://www.newspapers.com/image/104835050/.

———. "Local Man, Caught in 'Twister,' Lives to Describe Scene." March 19, 1925. Newspapers.com. https://www.newspapers.com/image/104828005/.

Johns, Robert H., Donald W. Burgess, Charles A. Doswell, Matthew S. Gilmore, John A. Hart and Steven F. Piltz. "The 1925 Tri-State Tornado Damage Path and Associated Storm System." *E-Journal of Severe Storms Meteorology* 8, no. 2 (May 4, 2013): 5-8, 16-18 https://ejssm.org/archives/2013/vol-8-2-2013/.

Kansas City Star. March 19, 1925. Newspapers.com. https://www.newspapers.com/image/655053482/.

Lashley, Sam. Interview with author. February 1, 2023.

Levins, Harry. "Author Recounts Day That Deadly Tri-State Tornado Hit Southern Illinois." *St. Louis Post-Dispatch*, September 5, 2014. https://www.stltoday.com/life-entertainment/local/books/author-recounts-day-that-deadly-tri-state-tornado-hit-southern-illinois/article_0e82f349-bd22-53ae-ae29-7aca219f9fa3.html.

Library and Archives Canada. "Personnel Record FWW Item." Government of Canada. August 30, 2022. https://www.bac-lac.gc.ca/eng/discover/military-heritage/first-world-war/personnel-records/Pages/item.aspx?IdNumber=481868.

Maddox, Robert A., Matthew S. Gilmore, Charles A. Doswell III, Robert H. Johns, Charlie A. Crisp, Donald W. Burgess, John A. Hart and Steven F. Piltz. "Meteorological Analyses of the Tri-State Tornado Event of March 1925." *E-Journal of Severe Storms Meteorology* 8, no. 1 (October 5, 2021): 1–27. https://doi.org/10.55599/ejssm.v8i1.46.

Marion Evening Post. "Eye-Witness Describes Terrific Tornado at Murphy." March 23, 1925. Newspapers.com. https://www.newspapers.com/image/756398572/.

Maryville Daily Forum. March 20, 1925. Newspapers.com. https://www. newspapers.com/image/87434446/.

McGee, O.E. "1925, Missouri Annual Reports of Public Schools; Advancement in Southeast Missouri." Missouri Department of Elementary and Secondary Education. https://mdh.contentdm.oclc. org/digital/collection/p16795coll16/id/13993.

McHenry Plaindealer. March 26, 1925. Newspapers.com. https://www. newspapers.com/image/167287971/.

———. "823 Dead, 2,990 Hurt by Tornado in Five States." March 26, 1925. Newspapers.com. https://www.newspapers.com/ image/167288120/.

Muncie Evening Press. "Flood Waters Are Nearing the Stricken City." March 25, 1925. Newspapers.com. https://www.newspapers.com/ image/250292620/.

National Archives. "The *Red Cross Courier*, Official Publication of the National Red Cross." April 15, 1925. 74236206.

Philadelphia Inquirer. "Hundreds Laid to Rest in Tornado Zone." March 22, 1925.

———. "7-Year-Old 'Sinner' Has Prayer Answered." March 22, 1925. Newspapers.com. https://www.newspapers.com/image/171069949/.

Pittsburgh Press. March 19, 1925. Newspapers.com. https://www. newspapers.com/image/150182085/.

Poplar Bluff Republican. March 19, 1925. Newspapers.com. https://www. newspapers.com/image/581310949/.

———. "4,000 Killed and Injured in Tornado." March 19, 1925. Newspapers.com. https://www.newspapers.com/image/581310879/.

Portrait and Biographical Record of Randolph, Jackson, Perry and Monroe Counties, Illinois. Chicago, IL: Biographical Publishing Co., 1894.

Princeton Daily Clarion. May 12, 1925. Newspapers.com. https://www. newspapers.com/image/437768197/.

Rushville Republican. March 21, 1925. Newspapers.com. https://www. newspapers.com/image/549409797/.

Salem Democrat. March 25, 1925, 1.

Sims, Jane. Phone interview with author. April 11, 2023.

Star Press. March 22, 1925. Newspapers.com. https://www.newspapers. com/image/251396882/.

———. "Latest Tornado Death List 848." March 20, 1925. Newspapers. com. https://www.newspapers.com/image/251396579/.

Stationery Office. "Supplement to the *London Gazette*." *London Gazette*, December 2, 1918. https://www.thegazette.co.uk/London/ issue/31043/supplement/14276.

St. Louis Globe-Democrat. "Cyclone Victims Panic Stricken Amid Desolation." March 19, 1925. Newspapers.com. https://www.newspapers.com/image/573010137/.

St. Louis Post-Dispatch. March 18, 1925. Newspapers.com. https://www.newspapers.com/image/140787673/.

———. March 21, 1925. Newspapers.com. https://www.newspapers.com/image/140787807.

St. Louis Star and Times. "Storm Destroyed Entire Village in 4-Minute Period." March 19, 1925. Newspapers.com. https://www.newspapers.com/image/204428843/.

Summers, John E. "West Frankfort Coal Mine Disaster." *JAMA: The Journal of the American Medical Association* 148, no. 9 (March 1, 1952): 713–15. https://doi.org/10.1001/jama.1952.02930090023006.

Sutton, Ann, and Myron Sutton. *Nature on the Rampage: A Natural History of the Elements.* Philadelphia, PA: Lippincott, 1962.

Testa, Adam. "Spirit of Historic Murphysboro Schools Lives On." *Southern Illinoisan,* April 7, 2008. https://thesouthern.com/news/spirit-of-historic-murphysboro-schools-lives-on/article_bd83df16-2f1a-575a-b1ed-058310959495.html.

Thomas, Mark. "Griffin Tornado." History as Prologue. April 16, 2013. https://dmarkthomas.com/griffin-tornado/.

U.S. Census Bureau. "1920 U.S. Census Report for Redford County, Missouri." n.d.

U.S. Department of Commerce NOAA-NWS. "1925 Tornado: NOAA/NWS 1925 Tri-State Tornado Web Site—Startling Statistics." https://www.weather.gov/pah/1925Tornado_ss.

———. "1925 Tornado: NOAA/NWS 1925 Tri-State Tornado Web Site—Weather Ingredients." https://www.weather.gov/pah/1925Tornado_wi.

———. "NOAA 200th Feature Story: History of Tornado Forecasting," October 4, 2023. https://celebrating200years.noaa.gov/magazine/tornado_forecasting/.

Wallace, Jerry L. "Address to the American Red Cross." Calvin Coolidge Presidential Foundation Inc. https://coolidgefoundation.org/resources/address-to-the-american-red-cross/.

Wayne County Journal and the Piedmont Weekly Banner. April 23, 1925. Newspapers.com. https://www.newspapers.com/image/588890806/.

Wichita Eagle. March 20, 1925. Newspapers.com. https://www.newspapers.com/image/720577404/.

ABOUT THE AUTHOR

J ustin Harter is a narrative nonfiction writer, copywriter and website consultant. He has written stories on General Ulysses S. Grant, southern railroads and distinguished bank robber Herman "Baron" Lamm that have been published in various regional publications. He has also worked as a genealogist, journalist and opinion writer for local newspapers.

Justin teaches coursework on design and copywriting at Indiana University and has produced pages and stories online that are read, seen and used by millions of people each year.

He lives in Indianapolis with his husband, Jeremiah. *The Great Tri-State Tornado* is his first published book.

Visit us at
www.historypress.com